UNDERSTANDING VALUES

A TREATISE BASED ON
MY PERSONAL EXPERIENCE

ABRAHAM A. GREAT

FOREWORD

Pastor Abraham Great was first introduced to me while I was working with one of the top pastors in Europe. I later found out that he is a man of great insights, multi-talented pastor and serial entrepreneur. I count it a great honour to write a foreword for this masterpiece - *Understanding Values*.

Understanding Values is a book designed for purpose-driven individuals that are determined to fulfil destiny. This book describes in clear and simple language the parameters you need for a fulfilling life here on earth. It also explains the level of importance that should be placed on each of these tools for life. Some of these essentials to life include praise, wisdom, gratitude, vision, the Bible's standard, thanksgiving, worship, positivity, self-discipline, money and an understanding of the will of God.

The author keeps the ideas in this book alive by backing them up with God's divine instructions from the Bible. The stories of men that fulfilled God's divine destiny for their lives are also incorporated to help the reader understand the application and implication of each of the parameters. The book tells what role a positive attitude plays in one's life and the consequences of having a negative attitude towards life in general.

The book intimates readers with the author's personal experiences in achieving God's given purpose for his life. It also narrates the processes he had to pass through to get to the point of internal and external fulfillment. This book reveals that everyone has a God ordained purpose for their lives, and a special gift given by God himself to every man or woman. This special gift is what defines the absolute value of the person. It is the discovery and achievement of this purpose that gives true joy and fulfillment in life. Thus the writer suggests that you find your God given purpose and discover your God given gift which will be your necessary tool to living a full and successful life here on earth.

Express instructions from the Bible are included to provide authoritative backing to the words of the author. It is also clear from the book, that man cannot progress or live a meaningful life without the help and influence of God in his or her life. God is the giver of life and has made available to everyone the necessary tools to living a life of progress and success, and these tools can be effectively harnessed by applying the principles provided in this book.

The book explains how any individual can find out the true will of God for his or her life and how to fulfill them. Knowing the true will of God not just for one's life but for every situation that may arise is relevant to achieving destiny. Time will not be wasted just going around the same spot and progress will become feasible.

It is in earnest expectation that as you read this book it will not only help you understand the requirements to have a great fulfilling life with God but also help others find the truth that you would have discovered within the pages of this book.

Gbenga J. Showunmi
Senior, Destinystar Ministries International
CEO, Cornerstone Creativity Group LLC
Houston, Texas USA

CONTENTS

DEDICATION

As always, I dedicate this book to my late father- **Rev. Joshua Olukunle Akintayo.** Your courage to withstand the cold hand of death when it struck your son at age 13: 'Undignified' in the eyes of those around that day, you set your feet dancing and prayed around the corpse.

Daddy, today your son is growing from glory to glory doing what you saw before you went 'home' to be with the Lord. I will always love you. Thank you for giving me the chance to live to fulfil God's purpose for my life.

ACKNOWLEDGEMENTS

Someone once said 'One is too small a number to achieve greatness'. I totally agree! For this reason, I would like to thank the team of people God has placed around me; those who have made it their goal to help accomplish my mission.

To my wife Queen - you remain the only person who is able to accommodate all my proclivities. You have always had the strength to do what I cannot do while I focus on what I can do.

To my Four Boys - your dynamism inspires me to write songs, books, articles and sermons. You guys are a good team in the' Great household'. I love you!

To all the staff and volunteers of GR8TERWORKS, HE LIVES BIBLE CHURCH, STR8T RECORD - you guys respond to my ideas and ideals without tiring - without your input, we wouldn't have had this manuscript.

To my father and role model, Bishop David Oyedepo: I am extremely grateful for the values you have taught, lived and continue to exude. You indeed are a man of value.

To my personal pastor, brother and great inspiration, Pastor David Oyedepo Jnr. - your wisdom is valuable for the accomplishment of my Divine Task - thanks.

To my hero, brother, great friend and mentor, Austin Jay-Jay Okocha - you are one of my best examples of living a life of value - I wish to share your wisdom with a lot more people who only know you by your skills in sport.

INTRODUCTION

Understanding determines the gap between ignorance, knowledge and wisdom... No one can regard something they don't know. Most people would live life being ignorant of important ingredients that could propel them into a better future. This book is written to help us see that there is knowledge to be acquired in all of our life's experiences. We don't only learn through education but we pick up valuable lessons from every situation and circumstance we find ourselves.

There is another group of people who know what these important ingredients are or at least some of them, but they seldom seek to understand how those ingredients could be implemented in their own lives in order to experience advancement. This book will help to connect dots, know how you can be pragmatic with the values you already know or even desire to have in your life. For example, many people understand that attitude determines your altitude. It's not enough to know it but do you understand the importance your personal attitude is having on your outcomes in life?

The journey with me in this book will help you develop the mindset for wisdom. Those who are wise not only are far from ignorance, but they have an understanding of the values that is required to manage their current moment, situation and circumstance. What we do with the moment can correct the past and create a more glorious future. Our outcomes are determined by our values. That's why making sense of life experiences could be a valuable skill for a person of value.

In 1997, I instinctively followed the voice in my inner man to leave my country of birth into uncertainty in another west African country. My parents and I only had contact details for an elderly Muslim relative whose phone number ended up being wrong. Basically I had no single contact. But what would await me from day one was just unimaginable. After 4 and half years in that country, I had become a celebrity, released an album in the French language and was a friend to several diplomats yet I was without a university degree. The amazing path was that an ambassador of one country could write a note to the to another embassy recommending me as a friend. When you decide to shift the dots, your life increase or decrease in value. My experiences have helped me understand and appreciate value.

Though I am publishing this book as part of celebrating my 40th anniversary on this earth, it contains pattern that my life could continue to follow however old I will become. Some of these values would be useful in your life too and I wait to hear your testimony personally.

The order of your life is glory.

It is working...

Abraham Adeshile Great

CHAPTER 1

VALUE OF A DECIMAL POINT

"It's not hard to make decisions when you know what
your values are."
—Roy Disney

It is commendable to want your child to be someone good,
but no one can become what they were not meant to be. In
a nutshell, what has not been supernaturally implanted in him or
her cannot be a part of his or her personality. Likewise, no one
can do, to the utmost, what they are not gifted to do.

WHO CAN DETERMINE THE VALUE OF A PERSON?

God, and, The person himself or herself – to a certain degree.
Human beings determine their worth themselves. 2 Corinthians
2:17 tells us,

*"For we are not, as so many, peddling the word of God; but as of
sincerity, but as from God, we speak in the sight of God in Christ."*

For instance, it is very hard to please a dreamer. What's more,
trying to please a man who likes change is a very hard thing. And,

the same can be said about a person who sees ahead of others. It is very hard to please somebody who refuses to settle for average. And I can say I am a hard person to please because I always think that we can do better as a church, than we are doing at this present moment.

I want us to understand that every human being has a special deposit from God and that whatever it is, it ultimately determines their value. In other words, what God has deposited on the inside of you determines how much you are truly worth. Do you know how valuable God has made you? Read Jeremiah 29: 11,

"For I know the plans I have for you, declares the Lord, "plans to prosper you and not to harm you, plans to give you hope and a future."

Also Job 8:7 says,

"Though your beginning was small, yet your latter end would increase abundantly."

And, 3 John 2 adds,

"Beloved, I pray that you may prosper in all things and be in health, just as your soul prospers."

I want you to understand that the will of God concerning us is bigger than we often dare to think. Likewise, our present achievements only signify the very least we can be as human beings. Some of us can pride ourselves in our academic degrees, a British or American passport etc. yet there's still much more to our lives than all of these things.

REMEMBER WHAT VALUE IS

Value refers to the relative worth, merit or importance. Ask yourself this question: How much am I worth? What is my merit or degree of importance? Let me also ask you: What value are you adding to your family, community or country?

Moreover, are you adding value to the Church and to the

Kingdom of God? Can God look at you and say, "This is my child who is pleasing to me?" Of what importance is God to you? I think that some of us; the only value God holds in our lives is based on how much we can get from Him instead of how much our lives are worth to Him.

Paul the apostle was someone whose life was so valuable to God that He had to step in to stop him from being murdered, on numerous occasions. Is your life currently worth anything? If you were to die today, would those left behind in your community feel the emptiness created by your absence?

I remember the time Steve Jobs died. I think that the whole world felt the loss caused by his death perhaps more than that of Michael Jackson. This is because Steve's was one of the most innovative brains this generation has ever had. Almost every household today can claim to have used at least one or more of his devices. But, being a person of value is not reckoned in monetary terms. So, I ask you again: what is your worth?

In case you are wondering, our worth does not depend on where we were born. If you were to be sold today, how much would you be worth in dollars or pounds? Real Madrid paid £18 million to buy Ronaldo; he broke the world record in football transfers at the time albeit some people feel it's only because he's a footballer but I won't delve into that debate right now.

Personally, I have always toyed, in my mind, with the idea of how much I am worth – overall – not just monetarily. I subsequently have come to the conclusion that if all I am worth is what I can see right now, then my life has not begun yet.

A lot of good things have happened in my life, but much more is yet to happen. Just to have a glimpse of my worth, I one time typed my name onto the Google search engine and I saw my books on Amazon. I discovered that people from different countries have bought them; individuals from about 13 countries.

So, through just my books, I've reached people that I have never met and may never ever meet in my life. Is that all I am worth, or can I possibly increase my value beyond what it is presently. The same applies to you; you are worth more than where you are currently though you may not realise it.

WHAT IS A DECIMAL POINT?

A decimal point according to mathematicians is a point or dot used to separate the whole number part from its fractional part. In fact, the same dot, written in a decimal number e.g., 8.674, or 45.6788, also serves as a full stop, placed between the integral and fractional part of a number; which determines the whole number.

I heard about the value of a dot, in a sermon preached by Pastor Mensah Otabil, an evangelical church minister based in Ghana. In this sermon, "the Value of the Dot," Pastor Otabil narrates the story of the man who is hailed in modern day medical practice as the best neurosurgeon ever – Ben Carson. This sermon hit me deeply on the inside and has since remained etched in my life. Because of this one message, I am very sure that my value (self-image) has been boosted significantly, and will certainly continue to do so.

As most people would know, Dr Ben Carson was the first Neurosurgeon in the world to successfully separate Siamese twins. Despite the challenges he faced growing up, this man has gone on to become the holder of the highest civilian award ever given in America; granted to him by former President, George W Bush, in 2008.

Dr. Carson is a specialist in separating conjoined twins, a feat that transforms people born in this condition, into separate individuals who then go on to become very active members of their communities. In short, he specialises in shifting decimal points. When you are 40, 50, or 70 years old, what do you think, in terms of what your personal value will be?

Do you envision yourself merely surviving on your pension? What exactly will be your worth? When your children are 25 years old, what will be their worth? Some people are smiling today because they have invested in their children. Others are wishing their parents would have invested in them more than they ever did. I am personally proud of my father because he instilled three things into my life and those of my siblings; things that I cherish immensely. These are:

1. Spirituality: My father imparted in us, a deep love for prayer; the fear of God and unbridled service to Him.
2. He made sure we were all well-educated, the best way he could. He always saw to it that we all had textbooks during school holidays, so we could read before term start. Plus, he often taught us, alongside the private tutor he had hired for us.
3. Health: Dad was always ensuring that we had access to good health. We all need it to fulfil our destiny.

How well have you been looking after your children's health or indeed their general wellbeing as a parent? How much are you investing into your own future and those of your children, in terms of quality education and godly training? Did you know, by simply changing your daily routines, lifestyle and habits, you are positioning yourself for constant change with regards to your life's value?

If, as the story goes, the young Ben Carson had remained a violent boy, there's no guessing what his worth in life would have been. For example, when you see a hoodlum; how much value do you place on him or her? On the contrary, if such a person decides to change, how useful do you think he or she would become to his or her community?

God has placed so much in us but what determines what we

make of it, is our daily habits and lifestyles, mostly. What is your daily routine like? I can also say that the kind of people you hang out with as well as the activities you get involved in, can determine your decimal point and your worth in life.

If you get yourself involved with people who are focused in life, you will become motivated too and that will in turn have a positive effect on your personal value in life. I certainly think that my value has immensely increased today because of the information I get from the great people that I associate with. Besides, I am still working on myself, to add more value to my life.

It is impossible to embrace the future if you are not willing to change the person that you are today. From the definition of the decimal point we got earlier, I can say that many people have stopped adding value to their lives. Some people stopped adding value the moment they went to school, some stopped after they obtained their first or even their second degrees.

The very place, at which you stop your personal development, is where your decimal point will be. Is your certificate your decimal point? Do you have to halt your personal development just because you got married? If, as I am sure you have noticed by now, a decimal point is simply a chunk of time, in human history as we know it, we can then safely conclude that that same period of time can be transient. So, in our personal lives, that fleeting time can also be either a full stop or a door way towards a different tomorrow.

I view all of my past, as just a fleeting moment in life and, I see my present and my future in the same way. What I am saying is; we must keep shifting our decimal point. We need to realise also that many others are constantly shifting their dot too. Let me ask yet again: Who are you? Are you the person that has now come to his or her full stop? Even as I ask, I am drawn through my mind's eye to a period in my life, when I didn't have a sense of purpose or destiny in this country; a period in which I was just a drifter in life – no status, no plans, no dreams and certainly no vision.

However, there are things we do because of the situations we may be facing at that particular moment; ones that would make it difficult for us to focus on a desired outcome because the past may have deeply shaped our lives, thereby restricting our freedom. Such restrictions often become the dot, for the rest of our lives.

I mean, someone may get pregnant out of wedlock and that pregnancy may put a dot on their lives, 'denting' their destiny forever, whilst another person may shake off the impact of that same misfortune and move forward without ever looking back.

What period are you in right now? Is it your full stop or are you still moving on? If you have not left that period, you have not changed anything! You are just surviving or simply craving to keep on moving forward.

SEVEN LESSONS FROM BEN CARSON'S STORY
Number One

Our entrance into this life is not determined by us. We can never decide how we are to be born or indeed our parents. Yet some people use their background as an excuse for not moving forward in life. Like I said, the best foundation for my personal worth was my family – my father to be precise.

But, I often wonder: what if my father had neglected us his children? I may not have been where I am today. Having said that, I still feel there was still much more my father could have done had it not been for some of the wrong choices he made in his life. I am very certain life could have been far much better for me. However, I can never lay any blame, in terms of my limitations solely on him.

I cannot use what my father did or did not do, as an excuse

for some of my failures in life. Please child of God, don't blame your parents. God knows what is best for us. The story of Helen Keller, for instance, would be another classic example of resilience in the midst of adversity. She developed a disease when she was an infant and it resulted in her becoming deaf and blind.

Her determined mother, however, got someone to teach her how to read and write despite her loss of sight. She went to university and became the first deaf/blind graduate to earn a Bachelor of Arts degree. Helen Keller ended up learning no fewer than five languages. She became one of the greatest women of her time in spite of the fact that she could neither see nor speak. She changed her decimal point! Remember, 99% of the rich people on earth today are from very humble backgrounds.

Number Two

We don't all start at the same level in life. In John 21:22 we read:

"Jesus answered, "If I want him to remain alive until I return, what is that to you? You must follow me.""

It is very telling, from Jesus' direct response here, that God wants each of us to be personally responsible for how we respond to the things that happen to us in life, without harbouring feelings of envy, resentment and/or contempt towards the people we think are faring better than us .

The onus is thus on each one of us; to choose whether we will always have a dot or a full stop in our faith. As I am sure you know; God's deals with us as individuals; as He prepares us to accomplish His purposes, in His Kingdom. Ben Carson was able to adjust his dot and full stop to the best of his God-given ability and so can you!

Number Three

Once again, our future is neither determined by our past nor indeed our present. It is not determined by where we will be tomorrow either – geographically or financially etc. As the saying goes, it is so easy to take someone out their native country than it is to take their nativity out of them.

Because many of us have the idea that we will at some point or other go back to our country of origin, this becomes a hindrance to our personal development in the 'foreign lands' where we find ourselves because we are still tied to the past. As for me; I am always forward looking.

I always look to the future, the way I visualise it and, I as a result always do what is necessary to motivate myself to live in the reality of it. Leave your past behind and stop the blame game! Start doing for your children what you could not do for yourself!

Number Four

No matter where we are in life, we can make that very place or circumstance, a starting point towards a better tomorrow. The decision you make today can make a difference in terms of where you end up in the next season of your life. You can this very day determine who you want to marry; you can even decide you want to change your life for the better, despite you not having control on your parentage. What we need to change in our life, is our commitment, prayer and work ethic.

Number Five

We can exchange what we have for what we need. For example, God gave each one of us the gift of 'time' and very often many of us do trade our time for something else yet the question is: do we make the most of our time? Likewise, we have talents and, the same way we deal with time, we can trade in our talents for something else, needless to say that most of us do not get to even discover what those talents are. Ben Carson discovered his talent and went on to become the recipient of the Presidential Medal of Freedom, at the White House, on June 20, 2008!

Number Six

A few minor adjustments to our habits or routines can create a big difference. In my case, change came into my life after reading Daniel 9:2:

> *"In the first year of his reign, I, Daniel, understood from the Scriptures, according to the word of the Lord given to Jeremiah the prophet, that the desolation of Jerusalem would last seventy years."*

Since then, I have become a 'book-worm!' I make sure I read at least twenty to thirty books, yearly! In fact, reading was one point of interest my wife and I shared, from the very start. At a certain point in my life, a decision I made to read not only my school text books but other useful books, has resulted into the person that I am today.

What you won't invest in yourself will not come out of you. Experts have posited that whatever you commit one hour to doing, every day; in five years you will become an expert in it. If you can get your son to play football for one hour every day, for five years, he will become an expert in that particular discipline.

Number Seven

God always gives us the opportunities we need to make the most of what he has given to us in life. See Matthew 25:14-30:

> *14 For the kingdom of heaven is as a man travelling into a far country, who called his own servants, and delivered unto them his goods.*
> *15 And unto one he gave five talents, to another two, and to another one; to every man according to his several ability; and straightway*

took his journey.

16 Then he that had received the five talents went and traded with the same, and made them other five talents.

17 And likewise he that had received two, he also gained other two.

18 But he that had received one went and digged in the earth, and hid his lord's money.

19 After a long time the lord of those servants cometh, and reckoneth with them.

20 And so he that had received five talents came and brought other five talents, saying, Lord, thou deliveredst unto me five talents: behold, I have gained beside them five talents more.

21 His lord said unto him, Well done, thou good and faithful servant: thou hast been faithful over a few things, I will make thee ruler over many things: enter thou into the joy of thy lord.

22 He also that had received two talents came and said, Lord, thou deliveredst unto me two talents: behold, I have gained two other talents beside them.

23 His lord said unto him, Well done, good and faithful servant; thou hast been faithful over a few things, I will make thee ruler over many things: enter thou into the joy of thy lord.

24 Then he which had received the one talent came and said, Lord, I knew thee that thou art an hard man, reaping where thou hast not sown, and gathering where thou hast not strawed:

25 And I was afraid, and went and hid thy talent in the earth: lo, there thou hast that is thine.

26 His lord answered and said unto him, Thou wicked and slothful servant, thou knewest that I reap where I sowed not, and gather where I have not strawed:

27 Thou oughtest therefore to have put my money to the exchangers, and then at my coming I should have received mine own with usury.

28 Take therefore the talent from him, and give it unto him which hath ten talents.

29 For unto every one that hath shall be given, and he shall have abundance: but from him that hath not shall be taken away even that which he hath.

30 And cast ye the unprofitable servant into outer darkness: there shall be weeping and gnashing of teeth.

Today you have another chance to determine your value. Besides, if you come across a person that you think holds the key to unlocking your destiny, I would say, go after that individual! If not, create a roadmap for your future and begin to search for that person that will help you access it. No time is ever wasted when one is in God's will. One of the richest men in the world today made his first million at the age of 69. So, anybody can make it as long as they are determined to bring about change in their life.

In the scripture we quoted above, Jesus tells different stories, including how a master distributed talents to his three servants… showing that God will not settle for anything less than the very best albeit His grace covers us in all our shortcomings. Furthermore, verse 26 in the passage above tells us why we have no excuse when it comes to the treasure that God has placed in each one of us.

I think it also tells us why some of us are where we are today; it is because we are not taking the steps we should, to foster our own personal development. We are happy to sail too close to shore, not wanting to take any risks. This is why the master was very angry with the servant who tried to come up with an excuse as to why he did not use his talent.

The words I want to lay some emphasis on in Matthew 25:14-30 according to the KJV are:

Talent: Talents are the abilities that have been divinely invested in us for the benefit of not only ourselves but others too.

Servant: We are all Servants of God because He has given us the ability and the gift of 'time.' What are you doing with your God-given abilities and time?

Ability: Ability implies one's level of competence i.e. what they are able to do. We all have different abilities yet I am aware that some of us have potential which we have refused to develop for various reasons.

Currently, in our church, I preach to a congregation of about a hundred people. However, I know I have the potential to preach to more than a thousand. Until your potential is developed fully, you are likely to regard it as merely an interest.

When you work on developing your ability, it will become a skill. Ask yourself what you have in you, right now that you can develop into a skill.

Gain: Gain means obtaining or securing (something desired, favourable, or profitable). It also means an increase in wealth or resources.

Trade: Trading is getting a thing in exchange for another. You can give up your time for something. If you are not satisfied with what you are currently getting, in exchange for your time, it's time for change.

Afraid: To be afraid means: "to be Worried that something undesirable will occur or be made to happen," - Merriam Webster Dictionary.

Risk: Some people refuse to shift their value because they are not willing to take risks. Look at it this way: The miracle of birth is a risk in itself. We come out of our mother's wombs at great risk, but once we are born we choose to become too cautious. Some of us have so many opportunities but we are afraid to step out of our comfort zones. Let us try to give our lives a push.

Talent: A Talent in the olden days was merely something to be admired like a trophy but today, its worth in various spheres of life is incalculable, even in monetary terms. Consider this scenario:

Ben's Talent: £50,000
Mary's: £20,000

Dennis's: £10,000

Now, let's assume all three of the above persons are in the same trade – fashion – they all design clothing. Let's also imagine that they all had the same mentor. I would imagine that after trying and trying harder, Dennis would at some point start to feel defeated in his heart and as a result quit making any efforts towards becoming a better fashion designer.

This is what some of us do! We look at other people, thinking they are better than us because they wear better outfits or drive better cars; a defeatist mind set! Nobody is responsible for your defeat, you are! You don't know their worth or value, but you have accepted that they are better than you. I said in the preceding paragraphs, your start point in life should not determine where you end up. Don't look at others; look at yourself. There is something of worth on the inside of you that just needs to shift.

We are coming out of this mind set in Jesus name! Where you live, who you know or don't, does not determine your future. You just need change!

I have noticed how a person's mind set often shows in his or her body language. Thus, we ourselves frequently determine where we place our dot. We can place our dot anywhere we want. There are so many opportunities around us, and if they are not enough, we can create more.

How do we create opportunity? Consider the following:
- Determine what you want in life.
- Determine what you want to get out of; what you are looking for. If it is training you need, go for adult education. There are courses you can do to enhance your skills.
- Invest in what you need to develop yourself. Acquiring a skill will definitely cost you money so set a goal for it.
- Don't only invest but also commit yourself to finishing it.

CHAPTER 2

THE VALUE OF WISDOM

"I may not be wise, but the beginning of wisdom is in me, the fear of God is it!"

A Story is told of a rich man who went to a certain place to solicit for some prayers. Besides this man, there were many others who had also come for the same. They were told God will answer them in turns. Having observed the situation closely, the man realised that it would take a while before he got his turn.

This was because by now, this man had found out what the requests of most of the people in front of him on the queue were. Having given his situation some further thought, he felt that he was able to handle most of the problems these people had. The needs these people, he thought, were quite mundane; everyday needs that he himself could easily meet instead of God.

Realising he could employ the jobseekers in his company, he told them all to leave the queue and wait for him outside, with a promise that he would attend to their needs. Truth is: he made these promises only because he wanted to gain quick access to God.

When he was asked why he was offering to employ all the

jobless folk he had met on the queue, he told them he was pursuing a business worth about £50 million, so, if God answered him he would easily sort out the other people's problems too. That is how some of us are.

We trivialise other people's problems to amplify our own. Always thank the Lord even if you have yet to become what you have always wanted to be. I know where you are, right at this very moment. There is nothing as bad as somebody remaining on the same spot for years.

Your story is about to change in Jesus name! How do you know you are making progress? It is when people that have known you for a long time find it hard to believe you are the same person they have always known all these years, because of the visible changes taking place in your life. Thank God! If it wasn't for Him being on our side, we would not be where we are today.

The value of any thing is sometimes determined by its scarcity. There are certain things you can get cheaply and others you can't because they are very expensive and scarce. With cars for example; it doesn't take long to see a ford being driven around, every day. The reason for this is simple: affordability. The majority of people can afford it. But how often do you see an Aston Martin being driven around? How many Bugattis have you seen this week? How many Rolls Royces?

I have used this example above to try and emphasise the value of wisdom. Knowledge can easily be accessed, wisdom is not. 2 Corinthians 2: 14 says,

> *"Now thanks be unto God, which always causeth us to triumph in Christ, and maketh manifest the savour of his knowledge by us in every place."*

The thing that stands between us and God is largely sin and possibly other problems of a personal nature. Even so, the grace of the Lord is upon our lives. We are being transformed even though we may at times not realise it. The grace of God is the reason why we are still alive today. At times we have been surrounded by people whose sole mission was our downfall yet God still grants us the wisdom to counteract those attempts. We should not be complacent because we seem to be making progress.

Proverb 4:7 says,

"Wisdom is the principal thing; therefore get wisdom: and with all thy getting get understanding."

Without wisdom, I would say, life is not really worth living. The principal thing in the journey of life is wisdom. It is an absolute necessity! Wisdom proffers the solutions to the many problems we tend to encounter in our day-to-day living. Remember I said earlier, knowledge is not the same thing has wisdom.

What you know about a situation is quite different from the way you go about dealing with it. How many people know that sin is an affront to God yet still go ahead committing it? There are so many things we know are wrong to do but we still do them, why? The answer is simple: lack of wisdom!

A BIBLICAL INSIGHT ON WISDOM

Proverb 4:3-9 says:

3 For I was my father's son, tender and only beloved in the sight of my mother.

4 He taught me also, and said unto me, Let thine heart retain my words: keep my commandments, and live.

5 Get wisdom, get understanding: forget it not; neither decline from the words of my mouth.

6 Forsake her not, and she shall preserve thee: love her, and she shall keep thee.

7 Wisdom is the principal thing; therefore get wisdom: and with all thy getting get understanding.

8 Exalt her, and she shall promote thee: she shall bring thee to

honour, when thou dost embrace her.
9 She shall give to thine head an ornament of grace: a crown of glory shall she deliver to thee.

In the above text, Wisdom speaks; it refers to God as its foundation, hence its instruction to the simpletons to: "Sell everything and buy wisdom". Some of us are traversing the journey of life with heavy loads. Trade them in for wisdom! The acquisition of wisdom should be top on our list of priorities, while we are on earth.

Ask God for wisdom and I can assure you, you will never regret it. It will add to your life. Never walk away from wisdom. As we grow in wisdom, we learn to build better relations with other people as well as getting the best out of those associations. Nobody can survive without people in his or her life.

On the other hand, if we lack wisdom we may find ourselves constantly having problems with people. A deficiency in wisdom is very often the reason why relationships get fractured. God places people around us so they can help us accomplish certain goals and vice-versa.

Wisdom helps us to make the most of every situation and circumstance in life. I consider wisdom to be man's interpretation of God's common sense. It is only common sense for God to give us solutions to our problems.

In other words, until God tells us what to do, we don't know how to go about doing it. The first level of wisdom is within us. For example, I have been praying for the growth of our church. God is telling me to first develop myself in wisdom before asking for growth.

If we have few people in the church now and their lives have not changed, what need will there be, for many? It would not be necessary to have them at all! The Word of God must first of all dwell in us richly. I believe this is the reason why God said I should present my heart clean first – Psalm 24:3-7

3 Who shall ascend into the hill of the Lord? or who shall stand in his holy place?

4 He that hath clean hands, and a pure heart; who hath not lifted up his soul unto vanity, nor sworn deceitfully.

5 He shall receive the blessing from the Lord, and righteousness from the God of his salvation.

I pray that God will give us all, the grace to apply ourselves to wisdom in Jesus name. If the outcome of what you think is your very best is not good enough, it is a sign that you need wisdom. If your best could not deliver to you, the desired solution, you need wisdom. Peter was a fisherman for years before he met Christ; he says in Luke 5:4-7:

4 Now when he had left speaking, he said unto Simon, Launch out into the deep, and let down your nets for a draught.

5 And Simon answering said unto him, Master, we have toiled all the night, and have taken nothing: nevertheless at thy word I will let down the net.

6 And when they had this done, they inclosed a great multitude of fishes: and their net brake.

7 And they beckoned unto their partners, which were in the other ship, that they should come and help them. And they came, and filled both the ships, so that they began to sink.

Notice how it was only after Jesus had asked Peter and his companions to cast their net into the deep-end of the lake that they caught a large school of fish. This is what it is like for most of us! We have toiled 'all night' yet without any success! However, when Jesus steps in, the outcome will be miracles!

When wisdom is applied to a problem, that predicament is done with, once and for all! Once, I was ministering in Nigeria when God revealed to Pastor Ayo Oritsejafor and Rev. Abraham Chigbundu, at the same time, that He was opening a ministry door for me, in Europe. Following that prophetic word, God linked me with people who assisted me to come to the UK, in ways that I can only describe as miraculous! One such person was the then Nigerian Ambassador to Ivory Coast.

There is a solution to every problem in this life. As Proverbs says, "wisdom is in the deep". Before we can acquire wisdom, we must search and pray for it. We cannot survive the journey of life without wisdom. The absence of wisdom in our lives makes us foolish because the opposite of wisdom is foolishness. Isaiah 5:13 says,

"Therefore my people are gone into captivity, because they have no knowledge: and their honourable men are famished, and their multitude dried up with thirst."

Also in Hosea 4:6 it says,

"My people are destroyed for lack of knowledge: because thou hast rejected knowledge, I will also reject thee, that thou shalt be no priest to me: seeing thou hast forgotten the law of thy God, I will also forget thy children".

Remember, you can know what to do but you may not know how to go about doing it. You may have the qualification as a surgeon, but you may get to the theatre room and not know what to do in a practical situation. A qualified lawyer sometimes may not know what to do for a given client. In order for you to deal with that kind of situation, you have got to seek the wisdom of those who know more than you do, in that particular field. So, get wisdom for it is the principal thing. Getting the best out of what you know, applying the knowledge to profit you and others; that is wisdom.

Getting the most valuable result out of every given situation is what wisdom is. You may be complaining about somebody always, but do you realise that with wisdom, the person you are complaining about; you can understand him or herself better? Luke 9:13-17 says:

13 He replied, "You give them something to eat."

They answered, "We have only five loaves of bread and two fish—unless we go and buy food for all this crowd." 14 (About five thousand men were there.)

But he said to his disciples,

"Have them sit down in groups of about fifty each." 15 The disciples did so, and everyone sat down. 16 Taking the five loaves and the two fish and looking up to heaven, he gave thanks and broke them. Then he gave them to the disciples to distribute to the people. 17 They all ate and were satisfied, and the disciples picked up twelve basketfuls of broken pieces that were left over.

In this instance, we can see that the people were hungry and Jesus asked His disciples, "What do we have?" The disciples responded saying, "we have nothing but five loaves of bread and two fishes," meaning they had only seven items all together. Why did they say nothing? Lack of wisdom! Jesus lifted the loaves and the fishes, up to God in heaven; He blessed the 'food' and right before their very eyes, the loaves and the fishes began to multiply.

The lesson here is this: when we bless the name of God for what we have, we can trust that He will multiply all our resources. Give God thanks, always! Don't allow negative words to proceed out of your mouth. You should never have to say, "I have nothing," because saying that is lack of wisdom.

Always operate with a mind-set of abundance and it will come to reality in your life. The scripture says, "Let the weak say, I'm strong…" The child of God should never entertain sickness; disease is not allowed in your body. Matthew 8:17 says:

"He took up our infirmities and bore our diseases."

We are not poor either because according to 2 Corinthians 8:9: Jesus has taken away all our poverty. Again, wisdom knows what to do or say at a given situation. The only way to confront the tough realities of life is to apply wisdom.

HOW TO MEASURE WISDOM

Wisdom is very often evident from what we do and say. I said earlier, wisdom can save us from shame, as it will always tell us what to do in any given situation. James 1:5:

"If any of you lacks wisdom, you should ask God, who gives generously to all without finding fault, and it will be given to you."

Ask for wisdom. How hungry are you in terms of your search for wisdom? Are you really hungry for solutions? Most of us only look for people that can solve problems for us, we cannot think for ourselves. In Psalm 45:1 the writer says,

"My heart is stirred by a noble theme as I recite my verses for the king; my tongue is the pen of a skilful writer."

If you list all your problems on paper, you can then turn them into questions because every problem is a question. Take the question to God and ask Him, "Lord, how can I overcome this?" Again, as scripture says, "if any man lacks wisdom let him ask." We need the wisdom of God to handle every situation and we need wisdom to survive – Proverbs 8:1-36

1 Does not wisdom call out?

Does not understanding raise her voice?

2 At the highest point along the way, where the paths meet, she takes her stand;

3 beside the gate leading into the city, at the entrance, she cries aloud:

4 "To you, O people, I call out; I raise my voice to all mankind.

5 You who are simple, gain prudence; you who are foolish, set your hearts on it.

6 Listen, for I have trustworthy things to say; I open my lips to speak what is right.

7 My mouth speaks what is true, for my lips detest wickedness.

8 All the words of my mouth are just; none of them is crooked or perverse.

9 To the discerning all of them are right; they are upright to those

who have found knowledge.

10 Choose my instruction instead of silver; knowledge rather than choice gold,

11 for wisdom is more precious than rubies, and nothing you desire can compare with her.

12 "I, wisdom, dwell together with prudence; I possess knowledge and discretion.

13 To fear the Lord is to hate evil; I hate pride and arrogance evil behavior and perverse speech.

14 Counsel and sound judgment are mine; I have insight, I have power.

15 By me kings reign and rulers issue decrees that are just;

16 by me princes govern, and nobles—all who rule on earth.[b]

17 I love those who love me and those who seek me find me.

18 With me are riches and honor enduring wealth and prosperity.

19My fruit is better than fine gold; what I yield surpasses choice silver.

20 I walk in the way of righteousness, along the paths of justice,

21 bestowing a rich inheritance on those who love me and making their treasuries full.

22 "The Lord brought me forth as the first of his works, before his deeds of old;

23 I was formed long ages ago, at the very beginning, when the world came to be.

24 When there were no watery depths, I was given birth, when there were no springs overflowing with water;

25 before the mountains were settled in place, before the hills, I was given birth,

26 before he made the world or its fields or any of the dust of the earth.

27 I was there when he set the heavens in place, when he marked out the horizon on the face of the deep,

28 when he established the clouds above and fixed securely the fountains of the deep,

29 when he gave the sea its boundary so the waters would not overstep his command and when he marked out the foundations of the earth.

30 Then I was constantly at his side.

I was filled with delight day after day rejoicing always in his presence,

31 rejoicing in his whole world and delighting in mankind.

32 "Now then, my children, listen to me; blessed are those who keep my ways.

33 Listen to my instruction and be wise; do not disregard it.

34 Blessed are those who listen to me, watching daily at my doors, waiting at my doorway.

35 For those who find me find life and receive favor from the Lord.

36 But those who fail to find me harm themselves all who hate me love death."

LESSONS FROM PROVERBS 8

Wisdom costs: in Proverbs chapters 1, 2, 3 and 4; we are shown that wisdom is from 'the deep.' Also see Proverbs 8 above.

Wisdom has company: When you find wisdom, it does not come alone. It works like a buy-one-get one free policy. Wisdom is always in the company of its friends. See Proverb 8:12 above. When you have wisdom, you become prudent. If you buy wisdom you become a person of honour; you will be able to foresee the future. Remember, the Bible also says "The fear of God means to hate evil…"

Wisdom does not make one popular, it makes one better: Its solutions to life's issues may not be met with general approval but it certainly makes things better. Therefore, don't look for acclaim; look for what will make God to be happy with you. A lady who goes into prostitution because she is in need of money has chosen a cut-rate solution, which does not make God happy.

That is not wisdom. Wisdom is the better approach. It's better to learn how to be more enterprising in life than to follow the route of waywardness.

Wisdom has many levels: A lot of problems can be solved with wisdom. On the other hand, having wisdom does not necessarily mean one will always make wise decisions or choices in life. Only God is capable of such. He says, "My ways are not your ways". Wisdom has dimensions and levels. God's wisdom is on a different level to man's.

Wisdom is better than gold: no mountain is ever insurmountable. If it seems that way, it is because we are in most cases, ignorant. What we don't know can kill us and ignorance is no bliss, as the saying goes. The story of the ten virgins in the Book of Matthew 25 comes to mind at this point: five had enough oil to keep their lamps lit, while the other five did not.

In verse 6: "In the middle of the night..." the virgins are told to go and buy themselves some oil. It's the same with wisdom. It is always available for one to buy. Whatever it is you think you cannot do, there is always somebody who has the knowledge of how it can be done. Henry Ford was not an altogether brilliant man – academically – but he was very wise. Whenever people wanted to embarrass him by asking him too many questions, he would always redirect those questions to his employees. As a result, people called him a dummy, saying he was too dependent on other people's ideas.

But, he very often responded intelligently; maintaining that he had employed people to solve problems for him, and not the other way round. He then would ask his critics if they could afford to employ people that can solve problems for them. He was further quoted saying that the reason why problems couldn't get to him; it was because he had a 'problem and failure manager' working for him. According to Ford, he could not talk about solutions, because he rarely knew what the problem was. This, in my opinion, is wisdom in action!

HOW TO FIND WISDOM

Somebody somewhere knows whatever it is you need in your life. That is why we all have to endeavour to read materials that can help us capture the things that we may otherwise not know. We need to sit down with people that have more experience than we have, and learn from them.

I used to go to the renowned Pastor David Oyedepo, periodically, to learn about church growth. Also, in the area of leadership, I am seriously reading John Maxwell's materials because he's an expert in that area. If you have a mentor, make use of the time you have with him or her wisely. I suggest you take the time to ask questions for the issues you may be facing at that juncture.

I have a friend who I find to be very cheap whenever I am looking for answers – "Google". If there's anything you are looking for, just type it onto Google, and this search engine will always have a related solution to it, for you. You can learn a lot from there. If you can spend 15 minutes to 1 hour on Google every day, I am you can perchance become as wise as Henry Ford was. Remember I cited Daniel 9:2 when I was discussing 'the Seven Things We can Learn From the Ben Carson Story.'

Google may not provide you with all the material you need so, I suggest you buy books to read as well. Stop giving excuses that you can't read or that you just can't find the time! Find an area where you need help and buy books that address that very area. Read those books diligently. If you become a reader, I guarantee you, you will become wiser. Reading enhances our intelligence. We need books to survive.

Romans 10:17 says,

"Consequently, faith comes from hearing the message, and the message

is heard through the word about Christ."

We absolutely also need the word of God. If books can solve our problems then the word of God can resolve them better than words penned by ordinary man. Remember Joshua 1:8 says,

"Keep this Book of the Law always on your lips; meditate on it day and night, so that you may be careful to do everything written in it. Then you will be prosperous and successful."

If you can take time to think, and I mean meditatively, you are guaranteed a positive result; you will be able to do better than you are doing currently. I have seen 'humble' businessmen and women building large houses and I have also seen heads of big fortune companies die as tenants. The difference between the two groups is as you may have guessed by now – wisdom!

What you have may not always be enough but it is your wisdom that determines what you do with it. The value you derive from life, determines your level of wisdom. Jesus had 12 disciples for 3 years and half years. From the original 12, the number grew to 120, and the 120 became 3,000 in just a day. You see, you have more than enough in terms of the resources to make a good start.

I know of someone who owned a car but who was always complaining about not having a job until a man of God advised him to start using his car as a taxi. He heeded the advice and went into the transport business. That one word of advice made him so rich that he even bought more cars in the end.

Lord, give me wisdom and keep me from destroying what you have by your grace bestowed upon my life. Some people, through lack of wisdom, have destroyed what God has already done for them. God, give me wisdom to overcome the erroneous ways in my life. Many are operating in foolishness, because they live life by trial and error. God grant me the wisdom to live above blunders, so that I will not find myself in unmitigated tragedies.

Give us grace to appreciate the questions that life often

throws at us. When people around us misbehave; that, in itself is a question. When we are struggling with lack that is a question too! God give us the grace to confront every question in our life with open minds. I pray that the wisdom of God will come upon us today as a baptism that will leave us refreshed, in Jesus name. Amen!

CHAPTER 3

―――――――― ❧❧❧ ――――――――

THE VALUE OF VISION

"Dream lofty dreams, and as you dream, so shall you
become. Your Vision is the promise of what you shall
one day be. Your Ideal is the prophecy of what you
shall at last unveil."
― James Allen

There is a significant difference between ambition, worldly vision and divine vision.

Every product we buy has a manual. For us humans, the word of God is that manual. If you don't own one or don't even bother to read the one you have, I would say you have a disease. I am implying that you cannot successfully live a fulfilling life without studying and practicing the word of God. Believe it or not; you will not be happy or fulfilled in your life.

A very close friend of mine – Minister Dimeji – always says, vision does not necessarily make you a hero neither does it make you 'superhuman.' Unless that vision is divine, you cannot pin you every hope on it. In short, a divine vision does not originate with you. It always has God as its foundation, and only what is His will stand forever.

The vision of our ministry for instance; it is not mine, it is

God's. I recently read a biography from which I discovered that nearly everyone who has had great vision throughout history has always acknowledged God as their source and not they themselves. That is why we often see such people giving most, if not all of their wealth, to worthy causes.

I am always of the opinion that you cannot receive vision except through dialogue with God. The same way a woman needs to have sexual intimacy with a man to conceive and ultimately give birth to a child. Certainly, you can have an ambition; you can be inspired to do great things, but true vision is given by the inspiration of God. Job 32:8 says,

"But it is the spirit in a person, the breath of the Almighty, that gives them understanding."

Vision is easily imparted to people who pray and habitually study and practice the word of God.

These three things are the foundations of a God-given dream or picture. I think you will always have vision if you do these three things habitually. Do you know why? It is because God delights in having fellowship with His people. You know the more you spend time with your parents, the more they are prone to reveal the secrets of their hearts to you. The same with God: Study His word, get closer to Him, and He will direct you let alone show you the future of whatever it is He has called you to do.

At times God can give you a vision for a specific assignment yet that same task may not necessarily be your purpose in life. Your purpose is inextricably linked to the grand picture that God wants to accomplish for humanity, through that charge that He has given to you.

Take Mary as an example; She was already engaged to be married to Joseph, and to probably start a family of her own, when God decided that she would conceive by the power of the Holy Spirit in order to bring forth the Saviour into this world.

She was not 'praying' for a 'miraculous conception' before she even got to intimately know her husband. No such record ever exists, biblically or otherwise yet somewhere along the line; her destiny became ingrained in God's glorious and self-determining plan, for man's redemption. You see, God's grand plan can apply to even people who are not born again! For example, Steve Jobs, the founder of Apple, the American multinational technology company; what he received was a God-given vision. He himself may not have realised it but I believe God had chosen him to come up with all that expertise, during his lifetime.

So, the fact that God has used you to accomplish something for him does not necessarily mean that you know Him. God desires a deeper relationship with you. Take the story of Samson in the Bible as another example. His record shows a grave deficiency, on his part, so far as having a relationship with God is concerned.

The few times we see Samson in prayer is when he felt his life was in danger. Even so, we see that God still gave him the vision to deliver the people of Israel from the terror of the Philistines. Unfortunately for him, his focus was not so much on his God-given assignment as it was on strange women! He was not perfect yet he was God's choice.

In Genesis we read about the birth of Jacob and Esau. Even before the two boys were born, God said "Esau have I hated and Jacob have I loved." Thus God had already committed future generations of the Israelites to Jacob. Note that both Jacob and Esau had no part to play as far as their vocation was concerned. The plan was God's and His alone.

As far as vision is concerned, none is greater than the other. The size of my congregation will not determine the size of my crown in heaven. It is not how much I was able to do; it is how well I did with what God had asked of me that will matter in the end. Thus our focus should be solely on God. We cannot worship

God and still serve mammon at the same time. When God gives us an assignment, it will always appear bigger than we ourselves.

If your vision is something you can accomplish on your own, there is a possibility it may not be of God. God's vision is larger than you. Likewise, if your dream is such that the people around you find it hard to fully grasp it even after you have explained it in detail, it may be another indication that the vision is from God. If your wife or your husband does not understand it, it may be an indication that it is from God.

Lastly, a vision may be birthed through prayer and worship. Quite similar to being pregnant; it doesn't matter whether a woman is married or not; as long as she has sexual intimacy with a man, the result will very often be conception. The same can be said about spending time in prayer. Fellowship with God will quite often result in the birth of a vision. And, the authenticity of the pregnancy is not determined by how long one has carried it.

The vision of our church (He Lives Bible Church) for example, was revealed to me on January the 21st 1998, while I was in Ivory Coast, yet the church didn't start until the month of April 2011 – twelve years later! Thus everything to do with this ministry – the present as well as the future – was written twelve years before it ever came into existence. Besides, I showed the documents regarding this vision to my wife, the very first time we met. Also, the very first discussion we ever had, had to do with planning. I told her that at the beginning of each year, she must set a clear-cut goal.

Mind you, there is something called a 'progressive word.' What it simply means is this: God may show you what to do but still withhold how you should do that very thing. Think of Moses: God obviously gave him the 'what' which he later discovered was to lead the Israelites out of their bondage in Egypt but because he did not up to that time have the 'how' (God's strategy) he took matters in his own hands and killed an Egyptian.

This resulted in him going into self-imposed exile and remained there until such time that God was ready to reveal his plan as to how he was going to get His people out of Egypt, in spite of Pharaoh's averseness to do so (Exodus chapters 3; 14, 15). The reason why God does this is simple: He simply wants your collaboration, not your initiative! Your failure in this regard may result into your vision being aborted. Seek God; move closer to Him so and your vision will become reality.

Write down the vision that God shows you and wait upon Him for its fulfilment, because it will surely come to fruition. In 2005, a friend of mine, Mike Aremu, saw a vision in which he was ministering in my church. The vision, which he saw in 2005, came to pass in November of 2011. Waiting for the appointed time is important. I recall every year, Mike would ask me: "When are you starting your church?"

But, I had to wait for the appointed time. When it is time, God will let you know and He will not fail you. He will always provide you with all the resources you need to accomplish your dream. He will remove the existing barriers out of your way. God alone has to take the glory. Let people glorify the name of God through you, in the name of Jesus Christ.

CHAPTER 4

———— ❧ ————

THE VALUE OF GRATITUDE

"Let gratitude be the pillow upon which you kneel to
say your nightly prayer. And let faith be the bridge you
build to overcome evil and welcome good."
— Maya Angelou, Celebrations: Rituals of Peace and Prayer.

Are you someone who is always grateful? I know there
are things, circumstances or people that we don't feel
grateful for. These people may include even our spouses yet we
should always be thankful to God for putting them in our lives.
God has surrounded us with very beautiful people. The book of
Genesis 2 states that God made everything and it was good, and
for Adam, there was no other companion suitable for him, than
the one the creator had chosen for him - Eve.

You know the rest of the story; how God put the man to
sleep, to shape the woman out of his rib... It is therefore a very
good thing that you should thank God always, for giving you a
companion. Some people are craving and dying for a companion;
their prayers have not yet been answered in that area. Some people
have even killed themselves because there was nobody to talk to
when they were facing challenges. Are you grateful for the gift of

life? You just have to be grateful!

Whether you think of gratitude as thanksgiving that does not matter; what is important is to have a positive attitude towards the grace that we have received – which has added great value to our lives. That is how an attitude of gratitude works. When you are thankful, you demonstrate that appreciation in various ways. What matters is that it originates from the bottom of your heart.

Once again the etymology of gratitude is: 'having a feeling of thankfulness' i.e. gratitude is not only what is expressed through thanksgiving and praise or worship - it can also be expressed through one's attitude.

It is quite easy to spot ingratitude in a person, even when he or she is not saying a word. We have to show gratitude for all the things God has done for us at all times. That is why I always say that if God decides not to do anything for me again; He has already done so much in my life and I am thankful. That is just the truth.

A lady who is not a member of our church called me recently to tell me that she had just woken up with a strong urge to do something for me. So, she started, showering me with her prayers. She said she was praying for me because of what God had just revealed to her about me. She went on to mention a lot of things about me, both negative and positive.

She mentioned how she had observed that I focus too much on the work of God to the extent that I don't even care to listen to the negative things people say about me; that I am grateful enough to the One who called me… I Hope you get the point. Look, God does not call those who are perfect but He perfects those that He calls.

In case there is something you are saying about me, which may in actual fact be a lie or truth; the point is, I am now too focused on being grateful to God and what he has done for me, that I no longer pay attention to busybodies.

Be grateful for the gift of life. Thank God for the children He has given to you. Thank Him for your house and stop your relentless whining. Always remember to be grateful. In my case, there are times when I just take my kids in my arms and with a heart full of gratitude, I offer my praises to God for their lives. Some people complain because all their children are the same gender; they want both sexes in their family. Some have three sons and they make it look like God has not been faithful to them! They complain that they do not have any daughters.

I have four sons but that does not bother me at all! I am simply grateful to God for my boys. It would be nice to have a daughter, but that is the least of my concerns. All that I know to do is be grateful to God for the boys I have been blessed with.

If only some people knew the challenges that all married couples often go through, they would stop keeping count of all the wrongs their partners have committed. You can't keep stock of all the negative things that have happened in life. If anything, you better be thanking God that you have a life partner because there are many people out there who wish they had one.

A lady once said, in my presence; "I wish God could give me a man – any man!" And there you are, still complaining about the one God has given you. Likewise, there are people who wish they had a 'Pastor,' simply because they are 'Pastor-less,' meaning they don't' have a shepherd over their lives. I was in China a while ago and I heard of people in that country, who have never heard about Jesus Christ. The first time I was in China, I had a chaperone with me. When I mentioned the name 'Jesus,' the guy asked who He was and I said He's my friend who has turned my life around. Then he said, "That Jesus must be a very nice man." On hearing that, I first thought he was kidding, until I realised he was serious.

The poor boy had never heard about Jesus Christ, albeit he

had heard about God without knowing who He really was. I told him more about Jesus Christ and advised him to Google the name in the Chinese language on the Internet, if he wished to know more about this man.

The fact that we know Jesus Christ is a great privilege and we should be thankful to God for that. Some years ago, 1999 to be precise, I took a trip to a place called Kai, in Mali. Mind you, the people of this town don't wear clothes. They cover only certain parts of their body, leaving the others exposed. I was shocked to discover such people are still in existence in this day and age.

I was as a result very grateful to God that we have come a long way as a people, where I come from; we wear outfits at least. Also, between 1993 and 1995, a group of us went on a missionary trip to a certain village in the Republic of Benin, in West Africa. We were stunned by some of the things we saw and experienced. People would show up naked for a church service! It gave me another reason to be indebted to God for providing clothing for me and my family.

This micro-chip age that we live in has made us to take a lot of things for granted. Things like electricity supply and security are all being taken for granted, whereas in some other parts of the world people have to pray hard to get these things. In fact, in some parts of the world, some people hire 'prophets' and security men for their protection because they live in environments that can be best described as highly risky and unpredictable. So, please be thankful to God always. Besides, it is good if all you will hear about today is being grateful. I want to encourage you to remain thankful for each day of your life.

THE THINGS WE MUST BE GRATEFUL TO GOD FOR

Having an attitude of gratitude simply means acknowledging

God's goodness to you even when you cannot see what you requested from Him. You can still be grateful even if it gets to a point where you realise that what you are seeking from God is not forthcoming. That in itself is indicative of a higher level of faith. It is the level at which you make up your mind to be indebted to God whether He has granted your request or not.

GRATITUDE

We are to be grateful because God has chosen us. The Bible says many are called but few are chosen. Do you know the population of the world today, and the number of people who have been misled by wrong religious doctrines? Because the Lord has called you and you have accepted that call; you have every reason for lifting your voice in praise to His name, for opening your spiritual eyes.

We need to be grateful for the grace of God in the lives of multitudes of people too. What we call Divine grace, is simply unmerited favour. It is God doing for us what we cannot do with our natural power or ability. The Book of Revelation says we are more than conquerors; that is when we are winning a battle we are not even aware of.

If God were to open our spiritual eyes, to see the battles He has won on our behalf, I very sure we would jump in ecstasy, thanking Him for those same victories. Therefore, we should learn to be thankful for His favour upon our lives even when it is not apparent to us. A proverb in the Yoruba language says, "A child who is thankful for the favour he or she got yesterday will receive another."

2 Corinthians 12:9 says:

"But he said to me, "My grace is sufficient for you, for my power is made perfect in weakness." Therefore I will boast all the more gladly about my weaknesses, so that Christ's power may rest on me."

God has covered your nakedness. He has clothed you with strength, and He has helped you in times of shame, when you would have been exposed; where you would have been caught or accused, He has released His grace upon you. Also, where people would have gathered to mock you, God has honoured you. So, why are you not thankful? Are you obliged to Him at all?

Lastly, we must be grateful for 'time' and 'chance', as Ecclesiastes 9: 11 says:

"I have seen something else under the sun: The race is not to the swift or the battle to the strong, nor does food come to the wise or wealth to the brilliant or favor to the learned; but time and chance happen to them all."

Psalm 127:1 says:

"Unless the Lord builds the house, the builders labour in vain. Unless the Lord watches over the city, the guards stand watch in vain."

Thank God for life. Thank Him for the chances and the opportunities that He gives to you. Thank Him all the time for your family, your future and for your career.

CHAPTER 5

———— ❧ ————

THE VALUE OF PRAISE

"I praise God because he not only guides my directions
but overrules my mistakes."
—Unknown Author

You cannot praise someone for what he or she is not able
to do. Allow me to start by saying that everything God
does, He does it only once. After that, it is expected to reproduce
after its own kind, in seed form. In short, the future of all of
God's creation is always locked up in its seed! For example, God
created only one man - Adam, and from that one man, He took
out the woman – Eve. Since then, the whole world has been
populated by the offspring of this first couple.

God created us for the wonder of His praise. Besides, praise
is not only contagious; it has the power to produce wonders! It
is the seed that harbours your miracle, child of God.

Many years ago, I travelled to Nigeria with a certain young man
because I needed to attend to some personal matters at the time.
I left with a Word from the Lord that He was going to sort those
personal matters out. My intention was to stay in the country for
only three weeks. Alas, the three weeks came and went. Before I

knew it, I had been in Nigeria for three months and after that, it seemed as though time had come to a complete halt!

By the end of it all, I had spent eleven months in Nigeria! Undeterred though, I held on to the one word that says, "I will go before you and make the crooked ways straight." I am happy to say that God did just as He had promise. And, I learned a valuable lesson: One of the few things we can do in the midst of seemly impossible situations is to 'praise' our way out!

Dear Child of God, coming out of your present situation is possible if you know how to praise. Allow me to say that praise is a technical manoeuvre. When it seems as though there's nowhere for you to turn, praise is that act that will guarantee that you land in your place of desire.

Praise will always outwit the enemy especially when you are in the midst of the most difficult of circumstances. Some people say they are spiritual because they go to a very 'spiritual' or 'spirit filled' church, yet this has nothing to do with praise! Praise is simply a way of expressing our gratitude to God Almighty, period!

We established earlier that praise means appreciation or thankfulness. Let's now look at what worship is and how it is different from praise. Contrary to the belief by some Christians; worship does not mean singing of slow songs. True worship involves conformity to the will of God (Matthew 7:21).

To put it simply, obedience is the highest form of worship! Besides, we cannot worship without sacrifice. Take for example the case of Cain and Abel. Both took their sacrifices to God yet only one was accepted – Abel's – while Cain's was rejected. There's a simple lesson in this: worship before God cannot be feigned! He will not accept our worship if it is not done in truth.

It is not possible for one to be thankful and yet fail to worship God. On the other hand, someone may say "Thank You" but not really have a genuine feeling of appreciation. You will often see this in children. Give a child something and ask him or her to say thank you. That child may say thank you yet without truly feeling any form of appreciation for what you have just given to him or her.

But, you cannot worship God if you cannot be grateful for what He has done for you. That being the case, I can say without any fear of contradiction that you cannot truly praise God if you cannot worship Him. In a nutshell, if you don't really feel what you are saying, then you are not really praising God in truth!

As we praise God, we always ought to have in mind the particular reason as to why we are doing it. Remember, He is our God and He's been good to us. Take some time to reflect at this point. What has God done for you, throughout your entire life?

We should bear in mind that we ought to praise God for all of His dealings with us. If it weren't for Him always upholding us in His omnipotence, we wouldn't be here today. Some of us moan about the things we don't have, only because we don't realise that if it weren't for God's grace, we wouldn't have even the very small things we have today.

I remember, some years ago, on an evening, a small group of us — all men — came together to record my music album. We put together an ensemble of the best of musicians and instrumentalists there were par excellence and set up a night vigil. We did everything we could to ensure the recording was a success!

However, a few minutes into the recording, the electricity supply cut off and, the generator we had brought for this kind of emergency just wouldn't work! We tried everything we could to get some sort of lighting but to no avail. After a while, we decided we were just going to praise and worship God, from 11 p.m. till 4.30 a.m. the next morning, without instruments.

We were so passionate about what we were doing that evening. The room in which we were having the recording was sweltering with heat that we resorted to taking off our clothes, praising God to the point of almost passing out! It is a night that I will live to remember for the rest of my life and I am pleased to say that God has today lifted each individual who was in attendance that night.

I also recall how sometime in 1999, and again, this was in Nigeria, we were supposed to have a recording but, it was at a time when there was a nationwide strike by public service workers. Because of that, we could not get any vehicle to transport us down to the venue.

So, we decided we were going to walk instead, and off we went, praising God along the way. That very day, God spoke to me again, saying that I would never have to walk on foot for the rest of my life. After that, God miraculously blessed me with a car and ever since, I have never been without a car in my life and again, I praise Him for that.

God dwells and rules in the midst of praise. True praise and worship ascend to God like a sweet-smelling savour. I therefore decree, child of God, that on the account of your praise today, He will remember you and your family for good in Jesus name! Praise is a secret, which many people don't understand.

Even so, we all have a reason to praise, no matter where we find ourselves; irrespective of the challenges we may be facing at the time. We should not go quiet on our praise. It is when we are in trouble that we should use the power of praise to get out of the situation. Praise has the power to assault all of the enemy's plans against us. It says in 2 Chronicles 20:1-30:

1 After this, the Moabites and Ammonites with some of the Meunites came to wage war against Jehoshaphat.
2 Some people came and told Jehoshaphat, "A vast army is coming against you from Edom, from the other side of the Dead Sea. It is already in Hazezon Tamar" (that is, En Gedi).

3 Alarmed, Jehoshaphat resolved to inquire of the Lord, and he proclaimed a fast for all Judah.

4 The people of Judah came together to seek help from the Lord; indeed, they came from every town in Judah to seek him.

5 Then Jehoshaphat stood up in the assembly of Judah and Jerusalem at the temple of the Lord in the front of the new courtyard

6 and said:"Lord, the God of our ancestors, are you not the God who is in heaven? You rule over all the kingdoms of the nations. Power and might are in your hand, and no one can withstand you.

7 Our God, did you not drive out the inhabitants of this land before your people Israel and give it forever to the descendants of Abraham your friend?

8 They have lived in it and have built in it a sanctuary for your Name, saying,

9 'If calamity comes upon us, whether the sword of judgment, or plague or famine, we will stand in your presence before this temple that bears your Name and will cry out to you in our distress, and you will hear us and save us.'

10 "But now here are men from Ammon, Moab and Mount Seir, whose territory you would not allow Israel to invade when they came from Egypt; so they turned away from them and did not destroy them. 11 See how they are repaying us by coming to drive us out of the possession you gave us as an inheritance. 12 Our God, will you not judge them? For we have no power to face this vast army that is attacking us. We do not know what to do, but our eyes are on you."

13 All the men of Judah, with their wives and children and little ones, stood there before the Lord.

14 Then the Spirit of the Lord came on Jahaziel son of Zechariah, the son of Benaiah, the son of Jeiel, the son of Mattaniah, a Levite and descendant of Asaph, as he stood in the assembly.

15 He said: "Listen, King Jehoshaphat and all who live in Judah and Jerusalem! This is what the Lord says to you: 'Do not be afraid or discouraged because of this vast army. For the battle is not yours, but God's. 16 Tomorrow march down against them. They will be climbing up by the Pass of Ziz, and you will find them at the end of the gorge in the Desert of Jeruel. 17 You will not have to fight this battle. Take up your positions; stand firm and see the deliverance the Lord will give you, Judah and Jerusalem. Do not be afraid; do not be discouraged. Go out to face them tomorrow, and the Lord will be with you.'"

18 Jehoshaphat bowed down with his face to the ground, and all the people of Judah and Jerusalem fell down in worship before the Lord. 19 Then some Levites from the Kohathites and Korahites stood up and praised the Lord, the God of Israel, with a very loud voice.

20 Early in the morning they left for the Desert of Tekoa. As they set out, Jehoshaphat stood and said, "Listen to me, Judah and people of Jerusalem! Have faith in the Lord your God and you will be upheld; have faith in his prophets and you will be successful." 21 After consulting the people, Jehoshaphat appointed men to sing to the Lord and to praise him for the splendor of his holiness as they went out at the head of the army, saying: "Give thanks to the Lord, for his love endures forever."

22 As they began to sing and praise, the Lord set ambushes against the men of Ammon and Moab and Mount Seir who were invading Judah, and they were defeated. 23 The Ammonites and Moabites rose up against the men from Mount Seir to destroy and annihilate them. After they finished slaughtering the men from Seir, they helped to destroy one another.

24 When the men of Judah came to the place that overlooks the desert and looked toward the vast army, they saw only dead bodies lying on the ground; no one had escaped. 25 So Jehoshaphat and his men went to carry off their plunder, and they found among them a great amount of equipment and clothing and also articles of value—more than they could take away. There was so much plunder that it took three days to collect it. 26 On the fourth day they assembled in the Valley of Berakah, where they praised the Lord. This is why it is called the Valley of Berakah to this day.

27 Then, led by Jehoshaphat, all the men of Judah and Jerusalem returned joyfully to Jerusalem, for the Lord had given them cause to rejoice over their enemies. 28 They entered Jerusalem and went to the temple of the Lord with

harps and lyres and trumpets.
29 The fear of God came on all the surrounding kingdoms when they heard
how the Lord had fought against the enemies of Israel. 30 And the kingdom
of Jehoshaphat was at peace, for his God had given him rest on every side.

Note, "The fear of God came on all the surrounding kingdoms when they heard how the Lord had fought against the enemies of Israel..."

So, it was not only the subjects who feared but the Kings also. Likewise, you may be afraid of your situation even as you read this book. Everyone gets gripped by fear, at one point or another. Even the prime minister is afraid of something. In this passage above, someone brought a report to the king that an army was marching against him.

Fear may not always be a natural reaction to danger but it is common. What is the situation in your life right now that you are afraid of? Are you contemplating how to overcome that situation? You've been asking yourself all kinds of questions on how you are going to pull through? I want you to remember this today: God is at work. Fear not!

Going back to the passage above, in verse 6; why do we praise? We do it because praise brings down God's presence and when that happens, there is nothing that can hold Him back from performing wonders in our midst. I believe it is the quickest way to get into God's presence. As in verse 8-9, may the Lord help us as we praise Him today, in Jesus name!

We don't praise God for fun. When King Jehoshaphat praised God, he received help. God helped him to overcome his enemies. In case we have listed all that is against us, when we praise Him, He will come down in the midst of our praise to help us overcome them all. If we are riding on the praises of God, we will definitely get a predictable result – victory!

God is the 'smartest compass' ever. He is the 'fastest navigator' there is, and I can guarantee you, He is precise. God does not only get it right, He is that which is right. He is the one that created what we are looking for. No one can catapult us into the future faster than He can. There is nothing we are looking for that He did not create. Nothing we want that He cannot make.

In Him was life, and the life was the light of all men. Recall, the Bible says without Him there was nothing made that was created. In case we are asking God for what is not physically on earth right now, even then, we can trust He can still add it to the list of our expected breakthroughs. How many of us are fearful of life's situations at this very present hour?

We should not be afraid of the current circumstances. Do not Fear. Terror is a cheap commodity that the enemy dishes out to people. Did you know that FEAR is simply, False Evidence Appearing Real? The Devil is a liar and he's the father of all lies! He lies everyday but God says fear not, because He will come through, in the midst of it all.

He will eventually bring us out in spite of the fact that the problem has lasted much longer; it still has an end to it. I personally believe that praise accelerates God's promises to His children. The Israelites said they could not praise God in a strange land yet He was only asking them to sing the same songs they had sang before they were driven into exile.

If we cannot praise, then the enemy knows he's got us backed into a corner. There will always be external and internal battles that will surround our lives: marital, spiritual, family or personal issues etc. yet praise, is the only thing that will keep us on top of the world in those circumstances. Whatever the condition of your life today; I say, you are coming out victorious in Jesus name!

WHAT WE NEED TO KNOW ABOUT PRAISE
We need to understand that:

The battle is not ours but God's. At a meeting I attended recently, an Englishman gave me a word from the Lord. He said, "God wants you to know that the gates of hell will never prevail over you." Certainly I was going through trials during that period. In fact the Enemy has tried at various times of my life to fight me viciously but, I belong to the Lion of Judah and I am not afraid of anything! Child of God, say to yourself right now, "My father is the Lion of Judah; I will not bow before anyone or before anything else, other than to Him and Him alone!"

Whatever you are going through, praise is able to bring you out of it. Don't fear. Praise Him until something happens! Even if your money or dream is being 'stolen' from you; ensure your praise is not. Appreciation for what God is able to do is one of the reasons why Abraham became the wealthiest man, in his day. Remember, he was the first man to pay the tithe. Scripture teaches that Abraham obeyed God, to the extent of laying down his only son for sacrifice. So, herein is an example of praise and appreciation, directed at God, who gave Isaac, to Abraham.

Dancing or clapping alone does not constitute praise; these are merely outward expressions of praise. On the other hand, the fact that you 'praise' in church every day, this does not mean you are grateful. If you are not grateful, your praises cannot be given whole heartedly. Psalm 150:6 says,

"Let everything that has breath praise the Lord."

I personally think that winners are not always a product of a battle.

Based on my personal experience; there are different categories of winners: There are those who win through a fight; those who win through struggle and those who are just 'born winners.' Remember, the book of Revelation says we are more than conquerors. So, the easiest way to overcome as a Christian is to let the Lord fight the battles for you. When God is fighting for you, you may not even know it. Very often it is the people around you who realise just how victorious you are.

I mean the kind of situations where someone just calls to tell you they have decided to offer you the job, when you don't even remember applying for it in the first place. Besides, when you tell them you did not apply for it, they tell you it was somebody else that recommended you.

That's what I am talking about! Such things happen when God is working on your behalf. Listen to this, I went back to the hospital where a few months earlier the doctors had told me I was anaemic and some medications were prescribed for me, to stabilise the condition.

To cut the story short; I stopped taking those medications after a while and praise to be God, it's been five years now. Today, the same doctors are saying my condition is way above normal. I believe God has intervened! No one can say no, when God decides your victory. Scripture says except the Lord builds the house, they labour in vain that build it. I remember also the time when God instructed me that I should go to Ivory Coast.

I told my friends about it and some of them while looking at me rather suspiciously said, "there are better places in this world: London, France and even America, why Cote'devoire?" But, I didn't pay attention to their negative response because God is my Shepherd. He leads me to my victory. The Bible says, "Don't lean on your own understanding." Today, I look back on that trip and on the events that followed, and I can say that I am so glad I obeyed God's voice when he spoke to me that time, irrespective of what others were saying to try and contradict God's instructions to me.

It is important to involve God in everything we do. In 2 Chronicles 1:12 we are told,

"Therefore wisdom and knowledge will be given you. And I will also

give you wealth, possessions and honour, such as no king who was before you ever had and none after you will have."

When you fix your eyes upon God, He will always come through for you. Giving Him all the glory and praise is what God deserves, no matter the situation. When you do that, God will always respond with His blessing to you. Besides, it will take praise to maintain that same blessing.

THE ESSENCE OF PRAISE

We must know what praise really means;

We need to know what it does;

We need to engage in the act of praise

We need to become praise addicts.

Maybe you are asking: Why am I using myself as an example throughout in this book? Well, I believe that my life's story is a great testimony to others; I have become an embodiment of God's faithfulness and omnipotence. For example, I asked the pastor of the church I attended as a teenager to introduce praise and drama nights, in addition to the other ministries already in the church at the time.

He agreed and within a limited space of time, the church rapidly increased, from eighty members to about six hundred members; to the extent that we later had to relocate to another building because of this growth in numbers.

That is why I often like to bring people together to praise God. You can also do it; start inviting people to praise God, even within the confines of your own home. You can also do it all alone if you so wish. Give God praise in the everyday situations of your life. And, the more fearful the battle of life gets, the more you should intensify your praise.

Most of us have now replaced praise with complaints as well as moaning about the things we think we don't have. Honestly, as a pastor, I should be counting those empty chairs in the church that are yet to be occupied. But no! That's not what I see. What I see, is where God is taking us and the thousands of people He has promised me; that, among many others, is the reason why I am saying we should be praising Him, even today. Scripture says, "Let everything that has breath praise the Lord."

More about what Praise is:

Psalm 147 says:

1 Praise the Lord.

How good it is to sing praises to our God, how pleasant and fitting to praise him!

2 The Lord builds up Jerusalem; he gathers the exiles of Israel.

3 He heals the brokenhearted and binds up their wounds.

4 He determines the number of the stars and calls them each by name.

5 Great is our Lord and mighty in power; his understanding has no limit.

6 The Lord sustains the humble but casts the wicked to the ground.

7 Sing to the Lord with grateful praise; make music to our God on the harp.

8 He covers the sky with clouds; he supplies the earth with rain and makes grass grow on the hills.

9 He provides food for the cattle and for the young ravens when they call.

10 His pleasure is not in the strength of the horse nor his delight in the legs of the warrior;

11 the Lord delights in those who fear him, who put their hope in his unfailing love.

12 Extol the Lord, Jerusalem praise your God, Zion.

13 He strengthens the bars of your gates and blesses your people within you.

14 He grants peace to your borders and satisfies you with the finest of wheat.

15 He sends his command to the earth his word runs swiftly.

16 He spreads the snow like wool and scatters the frost like ashes.

17 He hurls down his hail like pebbles. Who can withstand his icy blast?

18 He sends his word and melts them; he stirs up his breezes, and the waters flow.

19 He has revealed his word to Jacob, his laws and decrees to Israel.

20 He has done this for no other nation; they do not know his laws. Praise the Lord.

We see here that praise is good and pleasing to God. Through praise, we really appreciate God for who He is. Let me ask: who is God to you? Praise Him for who He is to you. The place you give to God in your life will affect your attitude towards Him. Do you put Him on a pedestal?

Listen, my God is always an overcomer! He is Jehovah Jireh, Jehovah Sharma; He is everything I want Him to be and He will show up on our behalf in Jesus name! Praise is pleasant and you know why? It is because praise is a sacrifice!

When praise goes up to God, it is pleasant; that is why He gladly and affectionately receives it. When we praise God, we are doing absolutely the right thing. You can sometimes pray amiss, but I tell you when you praise, you won't have long to wait for an answer. Scripture says, "In His presence, there are pleasures forever." If you don't have 'a praise engine,' ask the Lord to give you one so that your mind, body, spirit, and soul will be generating praise. Ask the Holy Spirit. "The spirit of Him that raised Jesus from death lives in you..."

The Spirit will quicken your mortal body; He will help you to become a praise addict. I decree: after today, you will become addicted to praising God in Jesus name! Remember David was thrilled as he transported the ark of covenant into the City of David.

He was so full of joy that he danced before the Lord with his garments nearly falling off and his wife, Michal, rebuking him for it, afterwards. When you are praising God, death may come; sickness may come, even failure may come yet I can assure you; God will deal with them all, on your behalf.

Remember, God later dealt with David's wife – afflicting her with bareness all her life – for mocking David while he danced before his God. David's life was far from perfect and even God who sees everything knew it, yet it seems that David praised his way out of all the errors of his ways. He was a man after God's heart. That is what praise can do, and, we cannot quantify it. Besides, it is not equal to being a praise leader.

Moreover, praising God out of a sense of duty is different from praising Him from a grateful heart. Having an attitude of praise is also very different from merely possessing knowledge about a musical instrument. In short, the fact that you know how to play music does not make you a praise addict – you may just be a musician.

I always consider myself blessed because of the knowledge of the mysteries that God has revealed to me. I know for sure that God has delightfully graced me with a gift that can never be taken away – singing. It is my prayer that we will receive the grace; for our mouths to ever declare the praises of God, in Jesus name.

WHAT PRAISE DOES

From the scriptures we read earlier, we saw that praise gives us a spiritual edge over the battles of life. None of us has the power to win this battle on our own. God's Word reminds us: "Except the Lord builds the house, they labour in vain that build it."

Praise transfers battles from us to God. Shadrach, Meshach and Abednego said "the God that we serve is able to deliver us" in verses 15 to 18 of Daniel Chapter 3:

Now when you hear the sound of the horn, flute, zither, lyre, harp, pipe and all kinds of music, if you are ready to fall down and worship the image I made, very good. But if you do not worship it, you will be thrown immediately into a blazing furnace. Then what god will be able to rescue you from my hand?"

Shadrach, Meshach and Abednego replied to him, "King Nebuchadnezzar, we do not need to defend ourselves before you in this matter. If we are thrown into the blazing furnace, the God we serve is able to deliver us from it, and he will deliver us from Your Majesty's hand. But even if he does not, we want you to know, Your Majesty, which we will not serve your gods or worship the image of gold you have set up."

King Jehoshaphat was able to defeat the Moabites and Ammonites because he transferred his battle onto God; see 2 Chronicles 20.

Praise provokes God into action. Psalm 22:3 says,

"Yet you are enthroned as the Holy One; you are the one Israel praises."

I think that when we pray, God dispatches His angels to bring answers to us. But when we praise Him, He Himself comes down. I also think that when we offer Him praise, He smiles at us; to show His contentment with what we are doing. And, because we are doing the right thing, He starts to put things in place on our behalf.

Praise opens doors. Act 16:25-27 says:

About midnight Paul and Silas were praying and singing hymns to God, and the other prisoners were listening to them. Suddenly there was such a violent earthquake that the foundations of the prison were shaken. At once all the prison doors flew open, and everyone's chains came loose. The jailer woke up, and when he saw the prison doors open, he drew his sword and was about to kill himself because he thought the prisoners had escaped.

Child of God, I speak over your life today; every prison door will break open in Jesus name! Those obstacles will not be removed by anything else other than praise. Whenever my old friends and I meet, we tend to recount the many things God did for us in the past; we share testimonies and praise God all over again. Find an opportunity to call people and praise God, even if your voice does not sound sweet to you, God will still accept it.

Engage in the act of praise

The act of praise produces wonders; no situation in your life will require anything more than praise. Psalm 149:6-9 says:

6 May the praise of God be in their mouths and a double-edged sword in their hands,

7 to inflict vengeance on the nations and punishment on the peoples,

8 to bind their kings with fetters, their nobles with shackles of iron,

9 to carry out the sentence written against them—this is the glory of all his faithful people. Praise the Lord.

Also Psalm 68:1-4 says:

1 May God arise, may his enemies be scattered; may his foes flee before him.

2 May you blow them away like smoke—as wax melts before the fire. May the wicked perish before God.

3 But may the righteous be glad and rejoice before God; may they be happy and joyful.

4 Sing to God, sing in praise of his name, extol him who rides on the clouds; rejoice before him—his name is the Lord.

My friend, are you ready to rejoice? Joshua, a great man of God, also understood the secret of praise. See Joshua 6:20:

"When the trumpets sounded, the army shouted, and at the sound of the trumpet, when the men gave a loud shout, the wall collapsed; so everyone charged straight in, and they took the city."

As our instruments of music begin to resound before God's presence, today, I declare that this shall be a sound of abundance upon our lives and upon everything else that concerns us, in Jesus name!

The secret that will enable us to take over our cities lies inside our praises. The Lord will give us this city in Jesus name and we shall eat the best of this land. The very best of the jobs this country has to offer will be ours in Jesus name. This nation will begin to yield increase for us in Jesus name.

Furthermore, I decree that there shall be a harvest of souls in Jesus name. Every door that has been slummed shut in front of us will open wide from now on, in Jesus name. What we have been unable to do before now; the power of God through our praises will activate the angel of God to start working on our behalf, in Jesus name. It says in Psalm 150:1-6:

1 Praise the Lord.

Praise God in his sanctuary; praise him in his mighty heavens.

2 Praise him for his acts of power; praise him for his surpassing greatness.

3 Praise him with the sounding of the trumpet; praise him with the harp and lyre,

4 praise him with timbrel and dancing, praise him with the strings and pipe,

5 praise him with the clash of cymbals, praise him with resounding cymbals.

6 Let everything that has breath praise the Lord.

Praise the Lord.

CHAPTER 6

THE VALUE IN PEOPLE

"About all you can do in life is be who you are. Some
people will love you for you. Most will love you for
what you can do for them, and some won't like you at
all."
—Rita Mae Brown

In Proverbs 27:21, the Bible says,
*"The crucible for silver and the furnace for gold, but people are
tested by their praise."*

This verse is about what people say about us – our overall
worth. If about three people are saying the same thing about you,
there may be an element of truth in what they say. In contrast,
more than a thousand people can gather and be saying something
wrong about you.

Psalm 2:1-3 says:

1 Why do the nations conspire and the peoples plot in vain?
2 The kings of the earth rise up and the rulers band together against
the Lord and against his anointed..,

From the preceding text, we can see that people can gang up
against us saying all kinds of unimaginable things but God will
deliver us from them all. Consider Joshua 24:15 as well. It says,

"But if serving the Lord seems undesirable to you, then choose for yourselves this day whom you will serve, whether the gods your ancestors served beyond the Euphrates, or the gods of the Amorites, in whose land you are living. But as for me and my household, we will serve the Lord."

My principle in life now is this: if God decides not to do anything for me anymore, He has already done so much and I remain thankful in this life and certainly in the one to come. As a kid, I was often terribly sick and hospitalised. At one time, a doctor certified me dead, and I was covered with a cloth in preparation for the mortuary.

My father ran into the ward from work, and when he saw me he striped himself naked in order to attract attention before starting dancing round my 'corpse'. The nurses ran away, thinking my father had gone mad because of what had happened to me. A doctor, by the name Kuku, was passing by; he saw my father and he called him by his name, "Rev Akintayo!" He knew my father very well hence his reason for stopping to sympathise with him. Additionally, the doctor held my hand as well as my father's. All of a sudden, he felt my pulse and yelled, "He's not dead!" That was how God raised me back to life. By the same token, there are so many visions and talents that have died before their time. But, I declare: you will live to see your dreams come true in Jesus name!

God values everything He created, including you. That is why I value every person our heavenly father has placed in my life. There are people who are now members of our church whom I have known for some years now, who can bear testimony to the fact that I value and love them genuinely from the bottom of my heart. It does not matter what people say about you, or what you are going through, I only see the best in you. I have come to challenge you today, to value the people around you. John Maxwell once said "People don't care how much you know until they know how much you care". If you have lost care for people, then you have lost the major part of you. I know a man who has the largest stash of gold any individual can ever wish to have.

He is a very wealthy man by the standards of this world. His native country is a member of the Organisation of the Petroleum Exporting Countries, (OPEC) and one of the richest countries in the world, yet this person sat on these this wealth for 42 years.

This is because in his eyes, a fellow human being was not worth nothing. On one of my trips to China; I watched an in-flight movie titled, "Devil Dump." This motion picture is a true life story of one of Saddam Hussein's son. This guy was brutally killing people; he was on hard drink and drugs. His behaviour, from what I saw in this movie, was appalling to say the least.

He stabbed his father's assistant to death. He abused ladies indiscriminately, and would kill them without a tinge of remorse. You may wonder, "Why did he do all these monstrous things?" The answer is simple. He did not see value in people. You and I may neither be Muammar Gaddafi nor Saddam Hussein, yet we kill people every day with our attitudes and sense of supremacy.

Everyone around us deserves to be treated with utmost respect. We need to learn to value people. Every child has value. A child who has never been hugged or appreciated will most likely end up as a hoodlum. There is a part of every human being that needs to be nurtured.

I am sure most of the people who are close to me have observed just how much I value my children. I hold them very close to me, telling them how much I love and cherish them. I am always proud of them, because they are my joy!

They also value me, which is why they tell me, "Daddy we love you, you are the best daddy in the world." Try to appreciate people around you, your husband, wife, and children. Let them know how much you love them, and how you are proud of them. If your partner says he or she is proud of you, it does not mean he or she is not aware of your weaknesses. He or she is just appreciating you for who you are. So try to see the best in your partner.

The essence of this series is to help us become an embodiment of higher significance. God has sent us here to raise a generation of people ready for the coming of our Lord Jesus Christ, and if you don't value people, you are simply not ready for it. Jesus places enormous value on people. We can see this from the story of the woman caught in the act of adultery, in John chapter 8.

When the people in the community gathered to stone her to death, Jesus asked if there was anyone among them who had not committed any sin before. He said, "Whoever has not sinned before let him be the first to cast the first stone." In spite of her short coming, Jesus Christ still saw the best in her. This is not to say He was in support of her sinful lifestyle; He was simply demonstrating how it is easy to turn around a person's life by showing them what they can become once they realise how valuable they are to God and his plans for each individual person.

Then there is also the story of the madman who lived in the tombs, in the region occupied by the Gadarenes (Mark 5:1-20); A man in whom the Lord Jesus Christ saw the best in spite of his mental illness. So Jesus decided to heal him of his madness. Even so, those who had no regard for human life became incensed that Jesus had healed this man on the Sabbath.

I pray that from now on, you will start to cherish and value people around you in the name of Jesus Christ. Don't try to get even with people! "I'm picking a fight with her because she offended me" or "I am picking a fight with him because he insulted me." What has an insult got to do with your destiny? That is not the standard of the Love Christ has for us. His love for us is unconditional.

It is an open-ended love. Some people are not able to achieve their destiny because they continue to dwell on the negatives in their lives. Everyone around me, including my wife, knows that if embarrassment is what it would take me to get what I am looking for, I would certainly condone it.

There was a day I was so embarrassed at the Monument-Bank Train Station, in London. I was singing praises to my God and got so carried away that I didn't realise people were staring at me with mixed feelings. I was so oblivious to the fact that people had gathered around me and were watching me in consternation. Worse still, some passing policemen saw me and stopped. One of them tapped me say, "Are you alright sir?" By the time I opened my eyes, the crowd that had congregated around had gone up in applause yet I was mortified because all eyes at the station were on me. I am saying I was embarrassed yet to be honest, I was not really bothered as I value my God more than anything in this world.

When you honour God, He will honour you in return. He will send you people who really matter, to honour you. He will provide all your needs and bless you with all the beautiful things you need to get by in life. Remember the Bible says "But seek first his kingdom and his righteousness, and all these things will be given to you as well."

The best way to acknowledge how much God is worth to you is to seek His kingdom at all times. Truly, when I look around me, I see that my significance has certainly increased because of my commitment to God. If being devoted to God increases our worth, then it means doing the opposite will deprive us this wonderful privilege.

If you don't value the people around you, you are simply forfeiting your own significance. We cannot grow up by your own standards and efforts, we need to identify with the truth of God's Word and acknowledge it in our own lives. The fact that someone has offended you does not mean you should wish evil on that person. Remember he or she is God's creature; created in the image of God. As a Christian, no matter what people do to you, you do not need to 'react' but you should instead 'act' in line with the commandment of God – to love.

God has given us a Christ-like heart as it is written in 2 Corinthians 3:18,

"And we all, who with unveiled faces contemplate the Lord's glory, are being transformed into his image with ever-increasing glory, which comes from the Lord, who is the Spirit."

Also, Psalm Chapter 18 reveals that the glory of God resides in every person we see around us; the only problem is that sin prevents it from manifesting in the lives of many people. It is good to look at people with the view of seeing only their best, instead of their flaws. We are killing them and condemning the work and glory of God in them if all we do is to put magnifying lenses on their weaknesses. Let us not be like the thief described in the Bible who,

"cometh not, but for to steal, and to kill, and to destroy…" – John 10:10.

The fact that someone within the church is not living in accordance with our expectations; whether he or she has had a child out of wedlock does not mean we should vilify that person. As a body of Christ, we must acknowledge every person's self-worth, irrespective of their character or status – without giving credence to sinful behaviour of course. Our core concern as the Church should be how we can help such people to start living lives that bring honour to the name of the Lord. You can partner with God to work on their lives with prayer and sharing the word of God.

A classic example is the story of the woman in Iran who rescued children suffering from the distresses of the war in that country. She saved their lives and through her influence they ended up becoming very strong Christians. Scripture does not permit to us to condemn or judge anybody. I plead with you to receive the grace to be your 'brother's keeper' in the name of Jesus Christ.

My prayer is that you will not only be a carer but that you will raise generations for God, in Jesus name. If a person's self-worth can be increased by the type of car he or she drives, or the house he or she lives in, how much more will they benefit from the significance that comes from having God in their life?

MORE ON VALUE

The definition of value is, "The regard that something/ someone is thought to deserve; the importance or preciousness of something/someone". It gives God pleasure, to increase us in worth as we hanker for more and more of Him in our lives. Allow me to repeat what I said earlier in this chapter. If we don't believe in people, especially those around us like our spouses and parents etc., it will be difficult for us to expect anything in return from them. There is no way we can get more from the people we don't value at all. The more you value individuals the more they gradually become pleasant to be around.

I will never forget this: It happen a few years ago when I was serving under someone else in ministry. I was leading Praise and Worship on a particular Sunday when the sole of my shoe came off because the shoe itself was cheap and of an inferior quality. But today, my story is different because God has blessed me beyond imagination. He has elevated me and added value to my life. Today I preach and people take notes, hallelujah!

The minimum number of people that God has promised me, with regard to the church that I am pastor of – He Lives Bible Church, in Milton Keynes - is a thousand! The people I see at the moment may be few but I can already see tremendous value in them; you are worth more than the thousands to me. I believe that God will take us to the level of a thousand strong congregation and even beyond, in the name of Jesus Christ.

If you don't believe in people then you are affecting their destiny negatively. Don't look down on people at all. In a few years to come, you don't know where God will have placed them.

WHAT DO PEOPLE MEAN TO YOU?

The moment you see more than one person, you are already looking at 'people.' The word "people" is generally used to describe two or more individuals. It could be a collection of men; women or children. The moment we see more than one person, they have, as far as I know, become a people. Where individuals are being counted and you happen to be there, you are definitely a part of the number to be counted – including the person standing next to you.

It is like the 'Law of First Mention.' The meaning of the law of First Mention is said to be the principle that requires one to go to that portion of the Scriptures where a doctrine is mentioned for the first time and to study the first occurrence of the same, in order to get the fundamental inherent meaning of that doctrine. Consider Genesis 1:22:

> *"God blessed them and said, "Be fruitful and increase in number and fill the water in the seas, and let the birds increase on the earth."*

We can see here the use of the word 'them' instead of 'he' because as you know, it was a while later that God 'created the woman – Eve – from the man's rib - Adam. Thus God blessed, future generations from just this one man –His blessing was on "them" (future generations) not just on "him" (Adam). God has placed value on people right from the beginning of the world. He already blessed future humans before they ever came into being; all their needs and all that would make them comfortable in life,

80

God created before He fashioned them.

Secondly, in Genesis 2:18-23 we are reminded that Eve was made from Adam. This is an indication that every human being is a product of another. We reproduce after our own kind. Therefore, anytime we look down on another person, we in actual fact look down on ourselves. Also, Genesis 6:1 shows us that every human being that God created is beautiful.

There are people who look at others and say, "Look how ugly this or that person is." That is not right at all. Try to be a blessing to others; think about other people, be considerate, and put yourself in their shoes. Don't look down on anybody; think of how you can assist that individual to add value to his or her life. Whatever God has given to you, think of how people around you can benefit from it too.

SEVEN WAYS TO HANDLE PEOPLE

Think of people. Avoid the go-it-alone syndrome. Remember, if you are surrounded by people, you are surrounded by helpers.

Let God to put you into 'a deep sleep' (like He did Adam) so that He can help you to develop good relationships through having a 'heart' for people. If God does not direct you, you are prone to start judging people wrongly. Matthew 7:1 says "Do not judge, or you too will be judged." No one is perfect!

See the people in your life as God's gift to you – they are a blessing from God – an asset – not a liability. See Genesis 2:22,

"Then the Lord God made a woman from the rib he had taken out of the man, and he brought her to the man."

The word I wish to highlight in this bible verse above is 'brought her to the man.' Eve was God's gift to Adam.

Respect and appreciate people. Be comfortable around people.

Sow love to the people around you, because in Matthew 22:39, the Bible says "Love your neighbour as yourself."

CHAPTER 7

———— ❧ ————

THE VALUE OF JESUS' STANDARD

"We should live our lives as though Christ was coming
this afternoon."
—Jimmy Carter

The Book of Proverbs 27:21 says,
*"The crucible for silver and the furnace for gold, but people are
tested by their praise."*
Joshua 24:15 also says,
*"But if serving the Lord seems undesirable to you, then choose
for yourselves this day whom you will serve, whether the gods your
ancestors served beyond the Euphrates, or the gods of the Amorites,
in whose land you are living. But as for me and my household, we
will serve the Lord."*

In this scripture, Joshua, boldly challenges the Israelites saying
that whether they serve the Lord or not, he and his household
would serve Him because Joshua knew the value of having God
on his side. I am here to let you know that there is only one
heaven, and it was created by God.

The standards set by God will always stand the test of time;
no one can get to heaven on their own terms. In the bible, we

read about a Nicodemus, a man who was very well versed in the Torah (Law of Moses); a ruler who went to Jesus to seek some answers on what one must do, to enter the Kingdom of heaven. Jesus made Nicodemus understand that,

"Except a man becomes born again, he cannot see the kingdom of God."

Jesus went further as to say,

"Except a man is born of the spirit and water, he cannot enter into the kingdom of God."

So here we are! Jesus works within the confines of His set values – not men's. In the gospel according to John, Chapter two, Mary the mother of Jesus went to Him, to ask if He (Jesus) could to do something about the wine which had run out at a wedding feast in Cana, at which they were both in attendance. Jesus responded saying: "Woman, why do you involve me, my hour has not yet come." So we see that Jesus himself understood the value of doing things within a set time. He had to wait for each event's appointed season.

Know this: no one can make it into the kingdom of heaven using his or her own standard and terms. Neither can you bring any one into the kingdom of heaven on own your terms, except you have created your own heaven.

Similarly, we cannot force people into the kingdom of heaven. Even Jesus, during His time here on earth; He did not force anyone into entering the Kingdom of God. No one will force you into the kingdom of God and no one will force Jesus Christ on you.

It is a matter of personal choice, but bear in mind that your choice will determine where you spend the rest of your life. You may be living a fun-filled life today, seemingly 'getting away' with anything you do, but remember, you cannot control heaven's judgment. You have to abide by the standards of Jesus Christ.

You cannot invent your own!

The value of Jesus' standard will guarantee you a life full of peace and joy with God. According to one of America's renowned leadership consultant, John Maxwell, "If we are growing, we are growing outside our comfort zone." What John is saying is this: If there is going to be a turning point in our attitudes or character in the way we serve God; in the way we live our lives and in the way others value us, it is not going to be on the basis of where we are right now. There are things we must do away with, and there are things we will have to avoid, which may be outside our comfort zone for this turn around to happen.

I have repeatedly said this to our church members: "if this church will grow; the growth will not happen within the boundaries of our comfort zone. We can expect that God will at some point push us out of our areas of ease." A short while ago, I looked at some strategies for church growth. I discovered that it is a costly venture – It demands thousands of pounds and countless hours of labouring. From that stand point, we must constantly try to adjust ourselves in order to achieve our goals.

You have to be willing to embrace uneasiness in order to move forward. You must sacrifice what you have not been able to sacrifice before. If your business will move to the next level; that growth will most certainly happen outside of your cosiness. Getting to the next level will call for a change in our sleeping and working patterns – we need a paradigm shift in our lives.

DEFINING A 'STANDARD'

The Oxford English Dictionary defines a 'standard' as "Something considered by authority or by general consent as the basis of comparison and approval model." It also means, "rule or principle that is used as the basis of judgement, or as average or normal requirement; quantity, quality, level and grade."

What is the standard of Jesus Christ, and what is its value? As Christians or children of God; His standard requires that we become Christ-like. We must then ask ourselves if we have been living like Him. Each one of us must ask him or herself this very important question: "Is my life modelled after Christ"? "Do people see Jesus in me?" In 1 Corinthians 3:11 we read,

"For no one can lay any foundation other than the one already laid, which is Jesus Christ."

As Christians, our foundation for conduct is only one – Christ. We should not idolise anybody, be it a Pastor or a Prophet, to the point of making them a yardstick for living. As a pastor, I am just a follower of Jesus Christ our Lord and Saviour, the epitome of all human virtue. He alone remains the definitive standard for us Christians. We are not to use human beings as a gauge for values.

Blaming our wrongdoing on another person does not make any sense at all. This is because the standard set by the Lord is unquestionable, and we will be judged only by our deeds. So blaming our misdeeds on others is foolishness.

1 Corinthians 3:9-15:

9 For we are co-workers in God's service; you are God's field, God's building.

10 By the grace God has given me, I laid a foundation as a wise builder, and someone else is building on it. But each one should build with care.

11 For no one can lay any foundation other than the one already laid, which is Jesus Christ.

12 If anyone builds on this foundation using gold, silver, costly stones, wood, hay or straw,

13 their work will be shown for what it is, because the Day will bring it to light. It will be revealed with fire, and the fire will test the quality of each person's work.

14 If what has been built survives, the builder will receive a reward.

15 If it is burned up, the builder will suffer loss but yet will be saved—even though only as one escaping through the flames.

I pray that we will not build in vain, in Jesus name. The Book of John 15:5 also says,

"I am the vine; you are the branches. If you remain in me and I in you, you will bear much fruit; apart from me you can do nothing."

The Kingdom of God is about fruitfulness. May your life be productive at all times, in Jesus name. Going back to 1 Corinthians 3:9-15: God is saying here that if we don't build according to the standard of Jesus, whatever it is we have been building (our way of life and message) will fail and we ourselves will suffer loss. By the same token, 1 Corinthians 6:9 says your body is the temple of Christ. And, Romans 12:1 says,

"Therefore, I urge you, brothers and sisters, in view of God's mercy, to offer your bodies as a living sacrifice, holy and pleasing to God— this is your true and proper worship."

Our life is a sacrifice to God. This message is unique because it is in line with my assignment in life, which is to raise a generation of people ready for the coming of Jesus Christ. Thus the question is: if Jesus Christ decides to come today, would you be ready to meet with Him in the air? If and when our lives are inspected, will they meet the standard set by Jesus Christ? From time to time, buildings need a lick of paint and refurbishment –at least every three or so years. If we compare our lives to a building, how often has that building been painted? What things are rotten in our lives that need eradicating?

Here is another one of Jesus' standards: in 1 John 5:3 He says, *"In fact, this is love for God: to keep his commands. And his commands are not burdensome."*

Ever since I read a book, by Jerry Savelle, about the golden rule, I have made up my mind that I will live the rest of my life correcting and improving myself on a daily basis. Keeping the *sins, in accordance with the riches of God's grace*

8 that he lavished on us. With all wisdom and understanding,

9 he made known to us the mystery of his will according to his good pleasure, which he purposed in Christ,

10 to be put into effect when the times reach their fulfilment—to bring unity to all things in heaven and on earth under Christ.

The lives that some Christians lead make unbelievers to run further away from God's kingdom. Matthew 4:1-11:

1 Then Jesus was led by the Spirit into the wilderness to be tempted by the devil.2 After fasting forty days and forty nights, he was hungry. 3 The tempter came to him and said, "If you are the Son of God, tell these stones to become bread."

4 Jesus answered, "It is written: 'Man shall not live on bread alone, but on every word that comes from the mouth of God.'"

5 Then the devil took him to the holy city and had him stand on the highest point of the temple. 6 "If you are the Son of God," he said, "throw yourself down. For it is written:

"He will command his angels concerning you, and they will lift you up in their hands, so that you will not strike your foot against a stone.'"

7 Jesus answered him, "It is also written: 'Do not put the Lord your God to the test.'"

8 Again, the devil took him to a very high mountain and showed him all the kingdoms of the world and their splendor. 9 "All this I will give you," he said, "if you will bow down and worship me."

10 Jesus said to him, "Away from me, Satan! For it is written: 'Worship the Lord your God, and serve him only.'"

11 Then the devil left him, and angels came and attended him.

If Jesus Christ could be tempted, what gives you the idea that you will not be? Let me repeat; Jesus Christ is our yardstick; the template on which to better our lives. The tempter will always come to us in different ways; it might be through the people around us or any other means. Such temptations will keep coming until we receive the grace to overcome those temptations. But if we are not patient, we may fail again and again. Everyone must be tried and tested, don't forget: the 'building' will be inspected. Whatever we have done and think nobody knows, the inspector which is Christ Jesus knows about it already. He is the owner of the building so He knows everything about it.

In the Bible passage above, Jesus Christ faced temptations in areas of His legitimate needs. Many of the temptations we face in life revolve around our valid needs, because we need certain things in order to survive. It is such temptations that lead many people into fraudulent practices or immoral activities such as prostitution and the like. Nevertheless, the Lord's standard still stands. With prostitution for instance; it is common knowledge that opposite sexes attract.

Even so, merchandising one's body for sexual reasons, despite it being a legitimate need, is not permissible. Not every need has to be met there and then and by all means possible. By the same token, just because we need money does not mean we should steal from others. God wants us to show the works of righteousness at all times. We should not fall prey to the tricks of the devil or indeed bow to him. The Bible says, "Ye shall worship no other God..." Anytime we yield to temptation we pay homage to Satan. See Matthew 4:6. Sometimes the devil will try to present us with opportunities that would make us prideful or even disrespect other people.

Jesus Christ resisted the sin of pride; He rejected everything the devil had to offer Him; He refused to 'flirt with temptation' in order to become a celebrity. Many of us will jump at every opportunity to become a celebrity, but little do we know that it is much better to be a hero for God than to be celebrated for something that is ephemeral.

commandments of God is the only proof that you love God and that you are a Christian and a child of God.

The best way to obey God is to adhere to His Word. Remember, 'all scripture is given for correction and for reproof.' If you hate correction, it means you hate the very thing designed to improve you or make you into a better person. Every football player goes for training on a daily basis no matter how good he is.

There is no other way for that player to advance himself in his career. As a believer ask yourself this question: "Am I living up to the ideal set by Jesus Christ for me to follow, or am I creating my own heaven?" God forbid that we should fail to make heaven; we have no excuse. The word of God is the standard by which all of us will be judged on the Day of Judgment, because the life that we live is not ours; it is supposed to be the life of Christ. See John 1:1-4:

1In the beginning was the Word, and the Word was with God, and the Word was God.

2 He was with God in the beginning.

3 Through him all things were made; without him nothing was made that has been made.

4 In him was life, and that life was the light of all mankind.

Also see Ephesians 1:3-10:

3 Praise be to the God and Father of our Lord Jesus Christ, who has blessed us in the heavenly realms with every spiritual blessing in Christ.

4 For he chose us in him before the creation of the world to be holy and blameless in his sight. In love

5 he predestined us for adoption to son ship through Jesus Christ, in accordance with his pleasure and will—

6 to the praise of his glorious grace, which he has freely given us in the One he loves.

7 In him we have redemption through his blood, the forgiveness of

In Matthew 4:8, above, at the end of the temptation of Jesus Christ, God sent angels to minister to Him because He had passed His test. Equally, if any of us passes their test, God will move us to the next level. We will encounter a turnaround in our lives and will move into a new season of productivity.

If you cannot enter God's Kingdom on your own terms, then you need to be aware that there will be a lot of external forces that will incessantly contend with you to stop you from entering it. The great Apostle Paul said, "The things that I do not want to do, I do, and those things that I ought to do, I do not do…" I therefore decree that everything that threatens your walk of 'freedom in God," in this season, will leave you alone, in Jesus name. Every weakness that has overwhelmed us in this season, will by the power of His anointing, leave us, in the name of Jesus Christ.

The anointing of God in this season will set us apart from all unrighteous activities, in the name of our Lord Jesus Christ. Would we rather be celebrated on earth at the expense of the promised everlasting bliss of heaven? I urge you; drop your own standard of living today and pick up the standard of Jesus Christ. Recall, the devil came to test Jesus in every way possible yet He responded with the Word of God. Correspondingly, God's Word is available for us to counter every temptation that we may face today. Do not overlook your weaknesses; it is the small foxes that destroy the vineyard! What you fail to conquer will ultimately conquer you.

CHAPTER 8

VALUE OF THANKSGIVING

"If the only prayer you said in your whole life was,
"thank you," that would suffice."
—Meister Eckhart

To take God for granted is to literally place one's self at a great disadvantage. One of the ways in which people take God for granted is by failing to thank Him for everything He has done in their lives. Remember how people came to Jesus saying we did signs and wonders in your name yet His reply was, "go away I never knew you."

When they wanted to know the reason why, Jesus' reply was, "When I was thirsty, you did not give me water, and when I was naked you did not clothe me." Still they asked, "When did we see you naked..." I pray that God will open our eyes to do the right things in the name of Jesus. He will open our eyes to see why we must remain thankful in Jesus name.

1 Thessalonians 5:18 says,

"Give thanks in all circumstances; for this is God's will for you in Christ Jesus."

Imagine a father who owns the whole world, stating in His

will that all he wants from his children is to be appreciated while they are expecting material things from him. The only thing God demands from us is thanksgiving and a heart of worship and praise. Anytime we refuse to thank Him, we violate scripture. The language of heaven is thanks and adulation. If we don't know this secret, we will always be banging on the pearly gates of heaven in prayer yet to no avail. In 1 Samuel 2:30:

> *"Therefore the Lord, the God of Israel, declares: "I promised that members of your family would minister before me forever." But now the Lord declares: "Far be it from me! Those who honour me I will honour, but those who despise me will be disdained."*

This is what happens when people take God for granted.

I think the reason why many are suffering in society today is because they don't honour God. Scripture says, "He that honours me I will honour." We can take a leaf from the nation of Israel. Every year, they have a month, specifically dedicated to giving thanks to God, for what He has done. For this reason God has appointed this seemly 'insignificant' country as 'prince' among the nations of the world.

This does not in any way mean that Israel as a nation does not have wayward people; it does, yet because the state was founded on the principle of thanksgiving, no other nation has been able to overtake her. God honours those who honour Him, and ridicules those who attempt to mock Him albeit we know from scripture that God cannot be mocked. When pride came upon King Nebuchadnezzar, God reduced Him to the level of an animal.

It is always wise never to sin against God. No one can stand His wrath. I have seen how as a result of our obedience, God is mightily prospering our ministry even though some people still cannot see these blessings. All they can see now is what they do not have, or the people they have invited but who did not show up.

As for me, I can see that God has done so much in my life.

God does not take delight in people who overlook the things that He has done for them (2 Timothy 3:1-9). Some people always want to attribute their success to their own ability, forgetting that it is God who created their brains who has given them that triumph – Deuteronomy 8:11-14.

For those who just cannot see anything good in life: There are a lot of people who have problems that are worse than the ones that are making you complain all the time but you know what? These people still find reasons to rejoice in the presence of God. We need to be people who are thankful and grateful at all times.

Gratitude will help us see our 'problems' as simply minor impediments in our faith walk. Remember God says we should be thankful in all things for this is His will concerning us. Gratitude provides us with easy access to God. If you want to move closer to God, you have to be grateful. That is heavenly protocol.

Remember the dictionary definition of Thankfulness we talked about earlier? Being thankful to God has very little to do with what we are feeling at any given moment. The fact that you say thank you does not mean you feel it inside of you. If we are thanking God, it must be from the bottom of our heart. The feeling must be from within.

WHAT IS THANKSGIVING?

Thanksgiving is expressing appreciation verbally. I am sure you know people who have certain disabilities such as vision impairment but despite their condition in life, they still remain happy and thankful to God. On the other hand, some people are not blind at all yet they never stop feeling depressed and complaining all the time. They complain about their wives, children, family members, friends, work and so on. Some even stop going to church because they 'did not' get the kind of miracles they wanted, at the time they thought they should have happened.

To be unthankful is actually sin. If you say thank you without feeling it, you have only made an empty speech. Thanksgiving is a sacrifice unto God. Psalm 100:1-5 says:

1 Shout for joy to the Lord, all the earth.

2 Worship the Lord with gladness; come before him with joyful songs.

3 Know that the Lord is God. It is he who made us, and we are his; we are his people, the sheep of his pasture.

4 Enter his gates with thanksgiving and his courts with praise; give thanks to him and praise his name.

5 For the Lord is good and his love endures for ever; his faithfulness continues through all generations.

Pride can make one not to appreciate God. Isaiah 12:3 says, *"With joy you will draw water from the wells of salvation."*

Joy is an expression of gratitude. It is besides, one of the gifts of the Spirit. It is also very different from happiness. Joy is constant – because the Spirit who gives it never changes; happiness is circumstantial. I think that the first prayer every child must be taught is the prayer of thanksgiving. Thanksgiving is the password that opens the gate of heaven according to Psalm 100:4:

"Enter his gates with thanksgiving and his courts with praise; give thanks to him and praise his name."

I thank that praise is the key for accessing every door in heaven. Learn to thank God with all your heart, at all times. Remember Jesus said,

"These people honour me with their lips, but their hearts are far from me" (Matthew 15: 8).

If you don't thank God daily, you have possibly missed His password for that day because His blessings are new every morning. Through my act of thanksgiving, God has given me some personal promises that I am seeing coming to fruition in this season of my life. Once I was thanking God for bringing me to this nation and He spoke to me saying "Because of this, I will establish you in this very nation." He also at the same time promised that I will forever 'possess' every country on which my foot will tread. Some people make excuses saying because they are still expecting one thing or another; they are not able to thank God. Open your mouth and appreciate Him today. He will do the rest for you in the name of Jesus Christ.

I think in addition to gratitude, praise and thanksgiving provide the quickest way to receiving miracles and blessings from God. If you want to see God at work, just go ahead and thank Him. Try to dance for the Lord, to the extent that you even sweat profusely. Stop being a 'sophisticated' Christian. The scripture says,

"I am the Lord your God, who brought you up out of Egypt. Open wide your mouth and I will fill it" (Psalm 81:10).

Also, Psalm 92 says,

"It is good thing to give thanks unto the Lord..."

Somewhere else the bible says 'give thanks unto Him morning and night.' If you look around you but still cannot find anything for which you can be appreciative to God; you are simply being insincere. No matter what is happening around you, God deserves your gratitude.

Don't let poverty to numb you to the extent that you cannot even bless God. Poverty has always been around since the fall of mankind and I believe will continue to be a source of the misfortunes of a lot of cultures across the world, till the end of the age as we know it. But, your gratitude can help bring about an end to those woes. One of the ways the devil makes Christians to lose their gratefulness is to magnify their problems.

But, it is at that very moment where you are told that your job has been terminated, that you should thank God the most. When you are confused and don't know what do; it is time to thank the Lord. That is your moment – carpe diem (seize the day)! Be a person who is grateful to God for life.

God has promised me a church of a thousand, and in my mind this matter is already settled. Some people still feel discouraged because they keep inviting people and those people don't turn up. Let us just thank God that we have mouths to use to invite people. This is what will make Him release His promises and His blessings to us.

We will thank our way into multiplication and into the envisaged multitude. In our ministry we don't muck about with our time of worship. Any ministry that takes worship and gratitude seriously will surely prosper and excel, to levels similar to those of the renowned Bishop David Oyedepo, of Nigeria.

Count what God has done in your life and be grateful. Also, look at what He is doing and count His blessings, every minute and hour. You will see that He has done so much already. Thanksgiving adds colour to our lives. It makes our lives meaningful. Of course life is not fair but it is our responsibility to add meaning to our lives. Gratitude must always be at the top of our 'to do list.' Those who murmur and complain always go about life in cycles. You want to reduce your blood pressure? Start by taking the daily dose of gratitude.

I watched a documentary recently that I found quite informative. The main thrust of this program was to promote gratitude. The presenters said the secret of wealth, happiness, and sound health is gratitude. Also, Oprah Winfrey once said that people should not focus on the negative things around them, they should rather be grateful for what they already have. No matter what goes on around us, we just have to be grateful.

Being appreciative will not only make you happy, it will possibly contribute to you living a long life, if you can make it a part of your everyday life. You can overcome any circumstances that may want to weigh you down in your spirit. Joy, gratitude and praise are the tools you need to do this. Don't let any day pass without saying "Thank You Lord." Psalm 67:5:

"May the peoples praise you, God; may all the peoples praise you."

How is divine increase linked with praise? If you can thank God even in the midst of a recession, I personally don't see the reason why you wouldn't prosper in those same circumstances. Be thankful! There is what I call the Fearful Dimension of God's Blessings. By this I mean there is a level of favour that God can take you to, that would absolutely scare you. Dear reader, God will take us to that level in the name of Jesus Christ. An example is Abraham in the Bible; he was so blessed that a whole nation could not sustain his wealth. Only praise can take one to that dimension of blessing. Cultivate the habit of thankfulness. Another classic example is Luke 17:12 which says,

"As he was going into a village, ten men who had leprosy met him. They stood at a distance."

Without even getting into a detailed exegesis of this passage, we can deduce the following:

The healing of the man who came back to show gratitude to Jesus was permanent. Remember, scripture says let the weak say I am strong (and as a song writer added, let the poor say I am rich). Let us always see His abundance; let us see beyond our present situation.

We must glorify God – always. The leper who turned back to glorify Jesus was made completely whole.

Cultivate the habit of falling onto your knees to worship him, every day. The secret of David's personal conquests was his ability to bow down and worship God with everything he had.

The thankful man in this story was a Samaritan - a stranger and possibly a sinner. Likewise, even if you are a stranger in the country in which you now reside , if you are one who knows how to give thanks, God can make you a blessing in that very nation.

Always return to God with a grateful heart, no matter the situation; always be cheerful don't be sad. The bible says we should give thanks in all things. And, In Mathew 15:36, Jesus gave thanks to God for the loaves and the fishes. Also, in John 11, he gave thanks for the life of Lazarus despite the latter having already been dead four days. God raised Lazarus back to life.

CHAPTER 9

———— ❧ ————

THE VALUE OF WORSHIP

"A little lifting of the heart suffices; a little
remembrance of God, one act of inward worship
are prayers which, however short, are nevertheless
acceptable to God."
—Brother Lawrence

The study text for one of the months in our church is 1
Thessalonians 5:18:

*"Give thanks in all circumstances; for this is God's will for you in
Christ Jesus."*

In Winners' Chapel, the ministry I was brought up in, negativity
of any kind is not permitted. I was spiritually raised with the belief
that in every situation you find yourself, you must always give
thanks to God. Even if you lose your closest family member, you
must receive the news, giving praises to the Lord. The time I lost
my dad, I went to inform the Bishop in charge. His response was,
"Praise the lord, Hallelujah; it is well." In that ministry, we give
thanks to God for literally everything! Also, we were not allowed

to feel offended, not to mention not forgiving others.

Some people say, "I cannot deny the fact that this or that thing doesn't go down well with me. The truth is: worldly reasoning, no matter how factual, can destroy one's destiny. The only fact I know is what God has promised concerning us. The scripture says let the weak say I am strong and the poor say I am rich.

It is very important to thank and appreciate God for His provisions in our lives – the air we breathe, the food we eat as well as the gift of life. Everything around us has been neatly packaged for us by God and we should always be thankful to Him for these things.

Would you believe if I told you that to keep a patient on oxygen for a week costs NHS £9,000? Yeah, that is how much it costs on the average. Now calculate the amount of oxygen God has been providing for us, freely, right from the beginning of our lives to date. Should we not value God for this alone? If we were to pay for the oxygen we breathe, from our current earnings; we wouldn't be able to afford it, would we? Even if we were paying in our local currency, we would have felt it still. What oxygen is to human beings is what worship is to God.

1 Samuel 2:30:

"Therefore the Lord, the God of Israel, declares: 'I promised that members of your family would minister before me forever.' But now the Lord declares: 'Far be it from me! Those who honour me I will honour, but those who despise me will be disdained."

For people who don't believe in God or indeed in the worship of Him; God says they are already condemned (John 3:18). Someone once said to me: "if there is a God, how come people are dying from various human woes, around the world?" I let this person know that nations have risen up, one against the other, right from the beginning of time as we know it; even before the Holy Bible was ever written. To this end, God said He will despise any nation that refuses to honour Him 1 Samuel 2:30

I saw on the news recently, two of the world's highest paid sports personalities – Johnny Wilkinson who plays rugby; who according to this cast was suffering from depression at the time. The other was the footballer, Carlos Tevez, who earns over £200,000 per week but who also ironically was said to be suffering from the same ailment as Johnny. Carlos's club and his manager even confirmed that he has a certificate to prove that he is a sufferer of depression.

This should tell us something: Money does not really add anything to our sense of personal worth. This is the reason why it cannot save one from depression. With all his wealth of ideas let alone his financial sway, cancer was able to get hold of one of the most innovative men in world – Steve Jobs – a sickness that led to his untimely death.

The scripture says, "What good is it for someone to gain the whole world, yet forfeit their soul?" Without worship, life becomes miserable. We are empty without fulfilling our primary mandate. God made us for His pleasure, which is to worship Him. Ephesians 1: 4-9:

For he chose us in him before the creation of the world to be holy and blameless in his sight. In love 5 he predestined us for adoption to sonship through Jesus Christ, in accordance with his pleasure and will— 6 to the praise of his glorious grace, which he has freely given us in the One he loves. 7 In him we have redemption through his blood, the forgiveness of sins, in accordance with the riches of God's grace 8 that he lavished on us. With all wisdom and understanding, 9 he made known to us the mystery of his will according to his good pleasure, which he purposed in Christ,

This chapter talks about why God made us. He made us for His glory. Every human being, irrespective of their complexion, has a primary mandate – worshiping God, period. In the Book of Romans 9:21, God says,

"Does not the potter have the right to make out of the same lump of clay some pottery for special purposes and some for common use?"

As human beings, we can put whatever we like in our homes for our pleasure. If we like, we can buy both air conditioning systems and heaters and decide to use them together all at the same time. That is our prerogative, no one can say otherwise.

But, a lot of people do not really worship God, they instead want to wrestle with Him; trying to prevent Him from having His way in their lives. However, God, in His will, predestined us for His pleasure. Heeding God's instructions should not be a problem to us at all. Some people worship God with tears in their eyes yet tears in themselves do not equate to worship. Total obedience to His commandment is what is important in life.

For those who are occasionally overwhelmed by sinful behaviour like David in the bible; He repented and obeyed God's commandment of praising Him whole heartedly. That is why there was nothing that God had promised David that He (God) did not do. If anything was wrong with David, God would straight away pull him up on it. And, David was always quick to acknowledge his wrong and to ask for forgiveness from God.

This is unlike most people. They can be caught sinning, but still deny the fact that they have done anything wrong. Are we truly worshiping God? I want us to choose today who we will worship. Joshua 24:15 says

"But if serving the Lord seems undesirable to you, then choose for yourselves this day whom you will serve, whether the gods your ancestors served beyond the Euphrates, or the gods of the Amorites, in whose land you are living. But as for me and my household, we will serve the Lord."

We have so many gods in the world today. Just like some worship football. Joshua said, "as for me and my house we will serve the Lord." I heard of a man who loved to pray, to sing and to listen to God's voice. He was very dedicated to his hour of worship. He religiously observed it every single day of his life. But as time went by, a dog he had bought began to disturb him during his times of worship.

So, he got a chain, in order to restrict the dog's movements during his prayer times. Thus the dog became used to being chained at that particular hour. Eventually, the dog stopped disturbing the master; it would instead at that very hour sit down to watch what the master was doing.

Interestingly, the dog later started doing whatever the master did. The master also had a child that used to observe what was happening. As the man was growing older, so did the dog and the child too. The child had been observing how the father used to bow down in front of the dog and how the latter would do the same as well.

When the child grew up and had had his own home and children, he decided to honour his father. So he too got himself a dog. He would tie the dog in front of him while bowing down to worship God. Then his children thought their father was worshipping the dog and so when they grew up they created a dog worshipping religion! They completely misunderstood what their father was doing! Choose ye this day, whom ye will worship.

FOUR AREAS THAT ADDRESS WHAT IT MEANS TO WORSHIP

Some people worship cows, some, their cars, others, football or news etc. Some people do not even worship anything at all. Some have never heard of Jesus Christ in their entire life. A medical doctor told me that they were trained never to believe in God or indeed any religion. Choose today whom you will worship.

Does God accept all kinds of worship? Some people believe

God will accept any type of worship. But, what is the value of true worship?

What or Who Do Many People Worship and how do they do it?

Hebrews 11:24-25:

24 By faith Moses, when he had grown up, refused to be known as the son of Pharaoh's daughter. 25 He chose to be mistreated along with the people of God rather than to enjoy the fleeting pleasures of sin.

In this text above, Moses refused to be called the son of Pharaoh's daughter. Had he allowed that, he would have been worshiping the gods that Pharaoh worshiped. Remember Jesus said give to Caesar what belongs to Caesar. Some people honour their president more than they respect God; for others its academic achievements or a British passport. Is that not pride? Their idea of God is the things they possess. Others prefer to be in a night club than in church, 2 Timothy 3:1-5:

1 But mark this: There will be terrible times in the last days. 2 People will be lovers of themselves, lovers of money, boastful, proud, abusive, disobedient to their parents, ungrateful, unholy, 3 without love, unforgiving, slanderous, without self-control, brutal, not lovers of the good, 4 treacherous, rash, conceited, lovers of pleasure rather than lovers of God— 5 having a form of godliness but denying its power. Have nothing to do with such people.

The passage above speaks volumes about what people will be like in these end times: 'Lovers of themselves, covetous, boasters, proud, blasphemers, disobedient to parents, unthankful etc.' Again, are we truly worshipers of God? What is the essence of calling yourself a child of God, if His image is not manifested on the inside of you? Pastor, it is not the size of your church or crowd that guarantees your entry into heaven. Similarly, it is not the number of miracles you perform. Scripture says many people will come to me on the last day saying, 'we did this and that in your name, I will say, "...I do not know you"... Why? It is because these people according to Christ are workers of iniquity. John 12:20 says,

"Now there were some Greeks among those who went up to worship at the festival."

It also says in 2 Thessalonians 2:10-12

10 and all the ways that wickedness deceives those who are perishing. They perish because they refused to love the truth and so be saved. 11 For this reason God sends them a powerful delusion so that they will believe the lie 12 and so that all will be condemned who have not believed the truth but have delighted in wickedness.

Unrighteousness is the god being worshipped by the masses at present albeit they may not realise it.

DOES GOD ACCEPT ALL KINDS OF WORSHIP?

The answer to the above question is a resounding no! The fact that we cry during worship does not really mean anything to God. Even the accompanying 'sensations' may not necessarily make it worthy either, because God is not moved by the worship of the unrighteous. If you are worshiping God and you are a fraudster, fornicator or liar, thinking that God is unaware of your intentional and deceitful sinful life, God cannot accept your worship. He simply cannot be mocked! Let's not deceive ourselves. If you are living an unrighteous life and preaching against it, you are only deceiving yourself.

WHAT IS THE VALUE OF TRUE WORSHIP?

If you cannot be broken in the presence of God, if God cannot interrupt your sinful life, then your worship is of no value to Him – just like Cain's in the bible. I know it is very hard for the flesh to submit, but through true worship, God is able to subdue your sinful nature and take control of your life. The grace of God is sufficient for us in the name of Jesus Christ. In Mark

7:6, the bible says,

"He replied, "Isaiah was right when he prophesied about you hypocrites; as it is written: "these people honour me with their lips, but their hearts are far from me."

As pastors, we can teach whatever we want to teach about God, yet we cannot bribe Him into accepting our worship if our lifestyle is contrary to His word. Sincerity alone will not work. It takes more than that! In the text above, Jesus said religious people were followers merely by 'lip service.' We cannot get to heaven by our own standard since the only heaven we have is built on God's everlasting standard.

AN INSIGHT INTO THE TRUE VALUE OF WORSHIP

Cain and Abel offered separate sacrifices to God, but Cain's was rejected while Abel's was accepted, why? God sees our hearts. It's just like the man who won a marathon but was denied his prize because he broke some rules during the race.

Do you know how painful that is? So, it will be when we get to heaven and God refuses us entry despite the number of years we claim to have served Him. Do you know if you are breaking any rules right at this moment? May His grace help bring about your turn around, in the name of Jesus Christ.

THE HIGHEST FORM OF WORSHIP

Obedience is the highest form of worship. When I was a teenager, God spoke to me; to leave my pursuit of a degree in Chemical Engineering, for the missionary field. He said He was going to send me to live in a country where the people would speak a language that I wouldn't understand. Miraculously, I got a ticket; I left Nigeria to go to Ivory Coast. And, just like He had promised; God assisted me, and I got free accommodation in that country; a place I had never visited before. Prior to my arrival in Ivory Coast, the Lord had revealed to me the person He was going to use to connect me to Winners' Chapel church in that country. He was the Pastor in charge. I was employed as the Music director, and God perfected everything concerning me because I had obeyed His command.

As I was about to start my ministry, God in the same manner spoke to me and again I obeyed Him. While man may not believe you, the voice of the Lord is always enough for you. Once you hear His voice, don't be so bogged down trying to get the approval of men. If you can't obey God, you can't serve Him in spirit and in truth. Job 36:11

"If they obey and serve him, they will spend the rest of their days in prosperity and their years in contentment."

Obedience means following the rules of God – Joshua 1:8. Have you been reading the word of God daily, lately?

Sacrifice: There was a reason why God accepted Abel's sacrifice: His sacrifice involved blood. Sacrifice is different from ordinary giving; sacrifice involves giving up of ourselves to God – to crucify the sinful nature in us. John 12:24 says,

"Very truly I tell you, unless a kernel of wheat falls to the ground and dies, it remains only a single seed. But if it dies, it produces many seeds."

Until you die to self, you cannot live for God. Paul says 1 Corinthians 15:31:

"I face death every day—yes, just as surely as I boast about you in Christ Jesus our Lord."

In Roman 12:1 it says,

"Therefore, I urge you, brothers and sisters, in view of God's mercy, to offer your bodies as a living sacrifice, holy and pleasing to God— this is your true and proper worship."

Place all your daily activities in the presence of God as an offering. I would rather not have a job than to work on Sunday, serving money as a god. I will serve God, because He matters to me a lot more than any other thing or anybody. God says, "Those who honour me I will esteem them." That is why my life is better than those that work on Sundays. If you find God, you have found treasures and everything that matters in life.

Forgiveness: The foundation of true worship is forgiveness. If you are the unforgiving type, you are not a true worshiper of God simple! An unforgiving spirit is an affront to God. God cannot be mocked. If there is anybody in your heart now, forgive and release that person. Colossians 3:13 says,

"Bear with each other and forgive whatever grievances you may have against one another. Forgive as the Lord forgave you."

Spirituality: Roman 8:6 says,

"For to be carnally minded is death, but to be spiritually minded is life and peace."

My spiritual father, Bishop David Oyedepo once said, "It is foolishness to be shameful of what is gainful." Some people think that I am too spiritual. I am therefore not surprised that they are still struggling with life till today. Spirituality offers me a lot of benefits; that is why my life is better than theirs. Why many people feel depressed is mainly because of their carnality. There is vitality in being spiritual. You should not be ashamed of church or anything that has to do with God.

Truth: God is a spirit and those who worship Him must worship in spirit and truth, John 4:24. Spirituality connects you with God. No one can leave my house in the morning without partaking in the morning devotion. Spirituality can lead you to your destiny faster than any other thing.

CHAPTER 10

───── ❦ ─────

THE VALUE OF YOUR GOD-ORDAINED PURPOSE

"More men fail through lack of purpose than through lack of talent."
—Billy Sunday

Paul wrote:
"*And we know that in all things God works for the good of those who love him, who have been called according to his purpose*" *Romans 8:28*.

The simplest definition of purpose according to the English dictionary is: "the reason for the existence of a thing." In the Greek, it is the word 'Prothesis' meaning a fore-ordained plan.

The said reality is that very few people on earth today, Christians included, know their purpose in life. And, it is very often obvious that of those who know, less than 5% have a written plan of how they want to fulfill their God-ordained purpose for their existence.

THE FOUR MOST IMPORTANT QUESTIONS YOU NEED TO ASK YOURSELF

From the beginning of man's history as we know it, mankind has been grappling with the questions:

- Who am I?
- What is the reason for my existence?
- Where am I going?
- How will I get there?

THE SEARCH FOR PERSONAL VALUE

The search for self-worth started with Adam and Eve and by extension, to this present generation of the human race.

In Philippians 3:12 (NIV), Paul says,

"Not that I have already obtained all this, or have already arrived at my goal, but I press on to take hold of that for which Christ Jesus took hold of me."

The King James Version puts it this way:

"Not as though I had already attained, either were already perfect: but I follow after, if that I may apprehend that for which also I am apprehended of Christ Jesus."

As the late Dr Myles Munro often said, "the greatest tragedy in life is not death, but life without a reason."

It is dangerous to be alive but not know why God gave you life. Similarly, one of the most frustrating experiences in life is to have time but not know what to do with it. God establishes man's purpose way before his existence.

God said to Jeremiah:

"Before I formed you in the womb I knew you, before you were born I set you apart; I appointed you as a prophet to the nations" (Jeremiah 1:5).

David also wrote,

"Your eyes saw my unformed body; all the days ordained for me were written in your book before one of them came to be" (Psalm 139:16).

This Search...

The search for self-worth is what causes people to do what they do. It should therefore be at the core of man's pursuits in life. It should be the director, in everything we do – for self, God and other people.

It is the reason why some people would betray their values or even religious convictions; the need to feel that they are something in life. This search or a lack thereof, is the reason why people commit suicide or even kill another human being.

CLEARING THE CONFUSION

The question in most people's minds is, "where do I start? Well, the bible says,

"Commit to the LORD whatever you do, and he will establish your plans" (Proverbs 16:3).

"Now when David had served God's purpose in his own generation, he fell asleep; he was buried with his ancestors and his body decayed" (Acts 13:36 NIV).

Note the three things David Did:

- He served
- God's purpose
- In his Generation

After he did all this – He died – was buried, and his body decayed. What a testimony!

What about you? What are you doing with your life?

Here Is a Reminder:

"To everything there is a season, a time for every purpose under heaven: A time to be born, and a time to die..." (Ecclesiastes 3:1, 2 NKJV).

One of life's greatest tragedies is to be a success, on a wrong thing.

It's not just about making every day count; it's about making your life count as well.

The bible summarises the life of Elijah the prophet as follows:

"Elijah was a human being, even as we are. He prayed earnestly ... Again he prayed, and the heavens gave rain, and the earth produced its crops" James 5:17.

FINDING YOUR PURPOSE: THE STARTING POINT

In Matthew 6:33 – we are told to 'seek first, the Kingdom of God.' And in Psalm 37:5 (NLT) the bible says,

"Commit everything you do to the LORD. Trust Him, and He will help you."

This should be your start point – seeking God's Kingdom, first; committing everything that you do, to Him. Remember,

"We are in this world but not of this world" (John 15:19).

YOUR GOD-ORDAINED PURPOSE IS DIVINELY LOCKED UP WITHIN YOU

Jesus stated in Luke 17:21,

"nor will people say, 'Here it is,' or 'There it is,' because the kingdom (rule or purpose) of God is in your midst."

The KJV puts it this way:

"Neither shall they say, Lo here! Or, lo there! For, behold, the kingdom (rule or purpose) of God is within you.

So, if God's Kingdom is within you, then His purpose (reason for your existence) is on the inside of you.

The God-ordained purpose for your life – including the entire plan for its completion as set forth by Him – is inside you at this very moment.

GOD HIMSELF WILL REVEAL IT TO YOU

"But when he, the Spirit of truth, comes... He will glorify me

because it is from me that he will receive what he will make known to you. 15 All that belongs to the Father is mine. That is why I said the Spirit will receive from me what he will make known to you." (John 16:13-15).

God works in your life through you – with your permission. There will be no one else to point to when you stand before Him to answer the questions concerning what you did with the life and purpose He ordained for you.

Paul wrote:

"For we must all appear before the judgment seat of Christ, that each one may receive what is due him for the things done while in the body, whether good or bad (2 Corinthians 5:10).

Most of us have a way of completing this sentence: "if God is God then…" Each of us has an unspoken, yet definitive expectation of what God should do. And when pain, failure, betrayal, rejection or loss come into our world, doubts begin to surface.

But, there's something you can do:

1. Start by Setting Goals

Goal setting is the process of matching your priorities or values with your dreams.

It is the process of choosing the direction and destination of your life.

If you choose being this it may exclude your being that.

The purpose of goals is to focus your attention. 'Anything will do' should not be the attitude of a child of God.

- Out of every 100 persons in America 33 have no real goal for their lives
- Of the 67 with a goal, only 10 have a strategy to reach it; they know where they want to go, but they don't have a clue how to get there.

115

- Out of these 10, only 2 will actually do anything about their goals to make them come true.

You should decide the quality of life you desire as well as the cost and commitment involved in that decision. (1Timothy 2:1- 5)

2. Determine the Value of your Goals.

Every set goal has to be accompanied by this one important question: where am I and how much?

You want to lose weight; how much?

You want to cut down on your spending; by how much?

You want to have kids; how much will it cost you, in terms of time effort and parenting skills?

I want to increase my income; by how much?

What will be the gain of your pain? GIVE YOURSELF A REASON FOR DOING WHAT YOU WANT TO DO. I WANT TO LOSE WEIGHT BECAUSE THE DOCTOR SAYS IT WILL LOWER MY BLOOD PRESSURE. (Describe the profit)

3. Let the Size of your Goals be decided by the Size of your God.

Make your goals so big that only God can fulfil them. You will never rise above your level of confession and vision.

Your attitude will determine your altitude. (Find a spiritual father)

The best dreams are those that happen when you are wide-awake and fresh from being alone with God.

In order to set the best goals in life do the following.
1. Visualise – the kind of person you would like to see in you, in the future.
2. People – you want to be around you. Remember, the bible says,

3. "Walk with the wise and become wise, for a companion of fools suffers harm" (Proverbs 13:20 NIV).

4. Consideration- the kind of activities you want to involve yourself in. Choose your battles carefully. You don't need to participate in just everything to make yourself feel useful.

5. Evaluation – are your goals a reality or not? I said earlier, it is a tragedy to be successful on a wrong thing.

6. Questioning – which of your goals are the most important and which ones are the least?

   Go against popular opinion – Even Columbus had trouble financing his ships for his "around" the world journey. Why? Because the people of his day believed that the earth was flat, and they were not willing to explore what lay beyond what they could see. Fortunately, Isabella, Ferdinand and Columbus himself ignored the experts. The Nina, the Pinta and the little Santa Maria set sail, and a flat world was found to be round. "Impossible" new lands became thriving and very "possible" places. This was because Columbus conjured up some ideas through vision and now his name remains in the chronicles of history. Hold nothing back, child of God. Go for your dream or vision and pursue it to the very end!

   Elvis Presley was turned away from his first ever audition; he was told he was only good as a delivery van man – a job he did before finding fame but look at what he went on to achieve in his life time. I am always of the opinion that the reason why people sometimes ignore you; it is not because you are not good at what you do; it's just because they don't know you, so take heart.

7. Pray – ask God about your goals. Are they contrary to his will? Are they pleasing to him? Our prayer lives always

reveal whether our goal is a real desire, heartfelt pursuit, or just a wish. Is it something worth praying for? Sometimes God delays an answer to prayer to see how much you believe in your dream, vision or God. Jacob worked 7 years for Rachel. Our prayer lives also reveal how much we are willing to be dependent on God as we work towards our dreams.

8. Count – the cost you will pay in order to achieve those goals. Failure to keep your mind on goals is the reason for shattered dreams. (Proverbs 23:7) What will be the pain of your gain?

9. Measure – the value of exchanging part of your life for each goal (Hebrews 11:23). Failure to achieve your goals or your dreams come true is more the result of wrong thinking than it is a divine plan.

10. Begin – the steps leading to the achievement of each goal. (Philippians 3:14)

CHAPTER 11

———— ❧ ————

THE VALUE OF A POSITIVE ATTITUDE

"Sooner or later the man who wins is the one who
thinks he can".
—Anonymous

*"Therefore, I urge you brothers, in view of God's mercy, to offer your
bodies as living sacrifices, holy and pleasing to God – which is your
spiritual act of worship. Do not conform any longer to the pattern
of this world, but be transformed by the renewing of your mind.
Then you will be able to test and approve what God's will is – his
good, pleasing and perfect will"* (Romans 12:1-2).

Think of the last time that someone spoke something
"difficult" into your life. Think about how you responded.
Did you react by taking offence and refusing to listen, insisting
that you were right and you had no case to answer? Or maybe
you felt hurt, but you decided to think about it and take it to God
with the attitude that says "What are you teaching me here, Lord?"

It has been said that "Your attitude determines you altitude." I believe this statement. Again, it is said, "Attitude is more important than aptitude." If we respond to our difficulties positively, determined with God's help to overcome, we will. If we react negatively with a defeated attitude, we will be beaten, no matter how brilliant we are.

Everybody has times when things go wrong. But when troubles come, it's not what happens to us, but how we react, that counts. Troubles destroy some people. Others they make. The difference lies in our attitude and what we do about resolving our problems.

The Church needs disciples with good attitude. It needs people who are willing to go, pray, serve, do. When things get tough, it's our attitude that determines whether we stay the course as disciples or whether we buckle under the pressure.

WHAT IS ATTITUDE?

Your attitude concerns the spirit or lack of it that you bring to a task, a person or a situation. Your attitude will determine your level of commitment, co-operation, reliability and perseverance. A football team with a positive attitude will come to a game with enthusiasm, good team spirit and a "never say die" approach. This kind of team will often come out winners over a team of more skilled players who lack team spirit and good attitude.

"If you'd like to win, but think you can't. It's almost certain you won't. If you think you'll lose, you've lost. For out of the world we find Success begins with a fellow's will – It's all in the state of mind." (Anonymous)

In spite of the fact that we know the importance of acquiring the right mental attitude, our entire educational system virtually ignores this vital factor. It is mainly directed at helping us to acquire facts with very little emphasis on developing attitudes.

Let's not make the same mistake in the church by concentrating on helping people acquire information and ignore our feelings and attitudes. A study by Harvard University revealed that 85 percent of the reasons for success, accomplishments, promotions, etc. were because of our attitudes and only 15 percent because of our technical expertise.

In any venture, attitude is of paramount importance, but especially in team activities. Since we have a vision of the church, which operates as "The Body of Christ" with all the parts interconnected and interdependent, it is of great importance that, as Christians, we come to the task with good attitude. Our attitude can determine whether the church succeeds or not.

"You've got to think high to rise. You've got to be sure of yourself before. You can ever win a prize" (Anonymous)

THE MEANING OF A 'GOOD ATTITUDE'

You have a spirit that is different from the spirit abroad in the world today. It means you are concerned about the affairs of God and his House, and not just your own.

You have been changed "in the attitude of your mind" (Ephesians 4:23). Remember if you can change your mind, you can change your life.

Your thinking resembles more and more that of Jesus Christ (Philippians 2:5).

You are prepared to suffer for the cause (1 Peter 4:11).

THE CONSEQUENCES OF A BAD ATTITUDE
1. It brings God's disapproval.

God was displeased with Solomon's attitude in 1 Kings 11:11 because he had not kept covenant. God threatened to take the Kingdom away from him. The lesson here is that a bad attitude can bring God's displeasure and it is possible for us to lose our inheritance.

2. You deprive the church of your gift.

Those with a bad attitude sometimes no longer wish to "play." If the ball is theirs, they pick it up and go home, thereby depriving the others. Those who will only play on their terms; those who are arrogant; those who wish to draw all the play to themselves end up resigning from the team or getting kicked out. In the church, such people withdraw their money, their talents and their time from the work of God, depriving the church of valuable assets. Worse still, sometimes they take others with them.

What about you? How is your attitude when the work loses its appeal, other Christians get on your nerves, and the church does not appreciate how hard you work for them? Do you take offence easily? When you don't feel that you are getting much for what you do, it's hard to keep giving your all, isn't it?

THE RESULTS OF A GOOD ATTITUDE
1. You have a "Can Do" mentality.

You are like Caleb in the Old Testament who was a man of a "different spirit." He saw things in a different light i.e. that the Promised Land could be taken in spite of the giants. You have a "can do" attitude. Jesus gave his disciples things to do rather than information to store away in their brains. The wonderful thing is that they obeyed him. Learning doesn't come by hearing but by being obedient.

2. You see that things can change.

You are like David who saw that Goliath could be killed with a stone and a sling. A good attitude helps you to see that your life can be changed and that your community can be different. Why go on complaining when you can change your attitude and actually do something about it.

3. You are willing to be submitted

One of the great problems in some churches is that the members want the Pastor to be submitted to them. The Elders or Deacons employ him, the membership have a vote. If he doesn't do as they say, he gets the sack. This is unbiblical and attitudes need to change. Father figures can only disciple their children if they are submitted.

Some have spoken of "terrorism" in the church, whereby the Pastor is intimidated and blackmailed into submission by threats to have him sacked, to walk out on him or to hold back finance. Others have spoken of the "church mafia" who run the church from the side-lines.

Hebrews 13:17 clearly says,

"Obey your leaders, and submit to them; for they keep watch over your souls as those who will give an account."

Submission is an attitude of heart, an attitude of respect and co-operation, an attitude of recognition of authority. If you have this attitude towards your leaders and if you are joined by a host of others with similar outlook, you have a church that can do great things for God. Of course, leaders also need to govern the church, not as dictators but as servants; not with an attitude of arrogance but with humility.

Success doesn't always go to the most skilled or the strongest but to the one with the right mental attitude. Neither does it always go to the one with the most knowledge or information. Skill, strength and knowledge are important, but add a good attitude, which has been formed by God's word, and you have all the ingredients for success.

CHAPTER 12

THE VALUE OF SELF-DISCIPLINE

"Perseverance must finish its work so that you may be
mature and complete, not lacking anything."
—James 1:4

Child of God here is a crucial challenge I would like to set
before you from the onset. Make a list of all the projects
you have finished over the past year. Now, list all your projects
that remain unfinished. Are you a finisher?

SELF-DISCIPLINE AND HOW IT CAN BE ACHIEVED

Self-discipline is one of the hardest qualities to achieve in
character formation. Having self-discipline means having the ability
to control yourself. To have self-discipline means "to continue
steadfastly in a course of action" (Oxford English dictionary).

A preacher once said that it means, "firstly to take hold;
secondly to hold on; and thirdly, to never let go." Beginning on the
road of discipleship is one thing, finishing is another. There is a
high dropout rate in every walk of life that demands discipline and

commitment. Even in Christian Ministry, there is a high dropout rate. Whether you finish or not depends on a number of things. One of these is certainly self-discipline.

According to an article in Reader's Digest, there are five qualities you need for success. Self-discipline is at the top of the list. The others are "bringing out the best in people," "developing special skills," "keeping promises," and "bouncing back from defeat." Irwin Hansen, an American businessman said that success depends, not on ability but on self-discipline.

He said, "All you need is a big pot of glue. You smear some on your chair and some on the seat of your trousers, you sit down, and you stick with your project until you've done the best you can do." In a long-term study of 268 American University students, many of them now over 65, it was found that those who were "steady and dependable" and "practical and organized" were far more likely to succeed in the long term than those who were "high-flyers" with enormous ability.

WHAT THE BIBLE SAYS ABOUT SELF-DISCIPLINE

In John 4:24, Jesus said,
"My food is to do the will of him who sent me and to finish his work."
Paul says, (Acts 20:24),
"However, I consider my life nothing to me, if only I may finish the race and complete the task the Lord Jesus has given me, the task of testifying to the Gospel of God's grace."
Writing to the church of the Corinthians Paul says, (2 Corinthians 8:11),
"Now finish the work, so that your eager willingness to do it may be matched by your completion of it, according to your means."
And James 1:4 adds,

"Perseverance must finish its work so that you may be mature and complete, not lacking anything."

Nehemiah, in building the walls of Jerusalem is also a good exemplary of self-discipline. Let us now look at some of the aspects we need to consider, to live a disciplined life.

MORE ON GOAL SETTING

1. Achievable Goals: When you set out on the path of discipleship, it is important to set yourself achievable goals. Goal setting is the first and most important step in making progress. Without any goals, it is very difficult to get far. So, before you start, be sure to set some targets or goals.

Reading a portion of the Bible, attending fellowship meetings, doing acts of service are all achievable goals that will help you on your discipleship path. You could work on imposing the voice of God (scripture) on the negatives of your life.

2. Desire to succeed

When you set yourself a goal, make sure that you have the hunger to accomplish it. What's the point when you do not have the desire to persevere? For example, you promised yourself that you would go to church every Sunday morning. But whenever the alarm clock rings, all you can think about is the work that needs to be done for tomorrow or the work you did yesterday that has made you so tired. So, what's the use of setting a goal in that case?

3. Perseverance

How often have we set ourselves goals and not achieved them due to some problem we meet? You see failure is part and parcel of growing up. But failure doesn't mean you have to give up. No! You must carry on, try again, and find out why you failed in the first place. Then try to achieve your goal again. You must persevere in spite of failure.

5. Take things one step at a time.

Finally, do not try to achieve too much at once. You must not rush things. When you have achieved one step, think about the next. Try not to think too far ahead when you have not even completed the first step. Slow and steady is the key here.

DISCIPLINE IN THE LIFE OF NEHEMIAH
1. He set himself a Goal.

Nehemiah set himself the task of restoring the walls of Jerusalem. Four times Nehemiah's enemies tried to distract him and four times he gave them the same answer.

"I am carrying on a great project and cannot go down. Why should the work stop while I leave it and go down to you?" (Nehemiah 6:2).

They were unrelenting in their efforts to distract him, but he was equally unrelenting in his determination to finish the work.

There will be attempts to distract you away from the goals you have set yourself.

- **You may experience a desire to be Independent.**

You may hear "voices" that ask you questions. "Why should I submit to Him (Jesus)?" or "Why should I submit to them (Church authority)?" Learn to silence these voices and to impose the voice of God (scripture) on them at an early stage of your walk. If you listen to these voices, you will become proud and stubborn and the Spirit of God will not rest on you. You will not allow anybody to speak into your life to help you. Joyce Meyer once said, "The dove always rests on the lamb." God dwells with those of a broken, submissive and contrite heart.

- **The Desire for Money.**

Jesus said,

"You cannot serve God and money" (Matthew 6:24).

128

You must make a choice and surrender greed to God. Many experience fear of being poor if they surrender to God. This fear in itself is a distraction and an enemy. Jesus said,

"See how the lilies of the field grow. If that is how God clothes the grass of the field, which is here today and tomorrow is thrown into the fire, will he not much more clothe you, O you of little faith?" (Matthew 6:28-30).

Learn to trust.

- **Conflict over Family.**

Many Christians today have been led into the mistaken belief that 'my family' comes before 'my calling.' Consequently, some may have a very relaxed attitude towards Kingdom work and they miss the voice of God in areas that are crucial to their development as disciples. I believe that we have been led into a "hierarchical" view of priorities which runs something like this - God first, family second, church third and others fourth. God sent you here on earth for a specific reason and as far as He is concerned, you must fulfil that purpose before your time here on earth is over. You might see that reason for your existence as your "Ministry, calling or purpose."

Nobody quibbles with God being first! However to put family over ministry, calling or purpose does not stand up in a scriptural sense. They should be put side by side, so that we are not exposed to the tyranny of the "either/or." They are both equally important and we should make room for both of them in our lives. A good disciple will organise his/her life in such a way that he gives time to family and also makes room for ministry, calling or purpose. Our mentality should be that of "and" and not "either/or" thinking. Of course, there will be times when we have to give time to one or the other but this should not be the norm. In the general course of events, I can give quality attention to my family at times other than Sunday morning.

- **Ambition**

Career minded people experience the same conflict and the same principle applies. Time must be made for that additional work but generally not at times that conflict with church events.

If you become distracted by any of these and fail to press on, there will be no harvest, no future blessing and no accomplished vision. On his way to discover America, Columbus was constantly threatened with the mutiny of his sailors if he did not turn back. Columbus refused to listen and each day entered two words on the ship's log, "sailed on."

Our spiritual enemies are sometimes unrelenting, but we must be determined to carry on. Can we write in our log at the end of each day "pressed on?" It is one thing to take hold of a vision; it is another matter to see it through. If Columbus had not sailed on, he would not be the man of destiny that he is today. Your destiny as a soldier of Jesus Christ awaits you and therefore you must not allow yourself to be distracted.

2. Nehemiah Refused to Listen to Lies.

If our enemies cannot distract us, they will attempt to lie to us. Nehemiah's enemies made up a story that he was planning a revolt and making preparations to be King. But Nehemiah would have none of it. He refused to start running around trying to justify himself. He had a vision that Jerusalem would no longer be a disgrace but a joy and a blessing. He knew that there was something great at the end of his endeavours. He simply replied that they were making it up and carried on working.

At the end of every race that is faithfully run; at the end of every project for God that is carried on with discipline and perseverance, there is a great reward. Firstly, self-discipline can give you a sense of self-worth. When you accomplish a goal, you will get a sense of achievement. Also having self-discipline can also boost your confidence that you can do more for God.

When you have confidence, things go more smoothly. You can also acquire new skills and knowledge. But most importantly, you are actually doing what God has made you to do.

CHAPTER 13

———— ❦ ————

THE VALUE OF MONEY

You may ask, "Why are you devoting a whole session to the subject of money?" The answer is very simple, because it is very important! Many would have the church avoid the topic altogether, because they think it has nothing to do with Christianity! They see it as the church trying to wheedle its way into their finances. Their attitude is: "My finances are my affair and nobody else's!" Here are some reasons why it is important to teach on money:

THE BIBLE HAS A LOT TO SAY ABOUT MONEY

Believe it or not, the Bible is full of references to money. Brian Sluth of the Christian Stewardship Association says, "There are 2,530 passages in the Bible dealing with money and material possessions – that's more than on any other subject - but it's the least talked about subject in the church. The church has been silent so long," he says, "that people don't understand the responsibilities that undergird a generous lifestyle." According to John MacArthur sixteen of the thirty-eight parables of Jesus deal with money. More is said in the New Testament about money than Heaven and Hell combined.

There is much misunderstanding and even resistance in this area. It is an area that actually defines the very nature and extent of our commitment to discipleship and consequently to Jesus. Billy Graham once said, "If a person gets his attitude toward money right, he will straighten out almost every other area of his life."

Generosity is a powerful life changing force that needs to be released from within each child of God. In other words, something dynamic happens inside you when you give! (Repeat memory verse). Richard Foster advises, "Just the very act of letting go of money, or some other treasure, does something within us. It destroys the demon greed."

The world needs to see a new model of church – a church with a positive testimony about giving rather than receiving.

PRINCIPLES IN DEALING WITH MONEY
1. The Principle of God's Ownership.

Psalm 24:1-2 says, "The earth is the Lord's and everything in it, the world and all who live in it. For He founded it upon the seas and established it upon the waters." This is the starting line for dealing with money. God is the owner. People are obsessed with their "rights." However, a disciple has no rights, only responsibilities.

Since God owns it all, we have no automatic "right" to money. We do have a responsibility to look after what is his and to use it as and when he directs. This can be frightening if we do not know our Father. God is generous, if we treat money as his property, then he will give us "all these things as well" (Matthew 6:33). His promise is that we will not be forsaken in poverty.

If God owns everything, he must be consulted in any major spending decisions. What car you buy, where you take your holidays, what house you buy and where, are all 'consultative' matters.

2. The Principle of giving God the first and the Best

If you have little money, the temptation will be to give God whatever is left over when you have paid for everything. In other words, you give God the last part of your income. However the in Old Testament, God taught the Israelites to always give him the first part and the best part:

"When you have entered the land the Lord your God is giving you as an inheritance and have taken possession of it and settled in it, take some of the first fruits of all that you produce from the soil of the land the Lord your God is giving you and put them in a basket. Then go to the place the Lord your God will choose as a dwelling for his Name" (Deuteronomy 26:1-2).

Read also Exodus 23:16, 34:22-26, Nehemiah 10:35, Proverbs 3:9. The Israelites were always encouraged to give not only the first but also the best.

With regard to money, we should decide to give God the "first" and not whatever happens to be left over. In the session on "Stewardship" we said that you need to give proportionately and systematically. In your budgeting, decide first what to give to God. This will release the blessing of God on the percentage that is left over. How much is the "first" part? This brings us to the issue of tithing.

Tithing was practised in Old Testament times and refers to giving 10% of your income to God. People say it no longer applies because it is inconsistent with being under grace. They say it takes the church back to Moses and the law of the Old Testament.

Firstly, it doesn't take us back to Moses; it takes us back to Abraham, long before the law was instituted. Secondly, grace is stronger than law; therefore we ought to give not only the tithe but also more than the tithe. If grace will move you in any direction from 10%, that direction will certainly be upwards.

Billy Graham, in his sermon "Partners with God," accused

America of robbing God. He said we do not start giving until we give a tenth "for it belongs to him already" (Leviticus 27:30). It is only after we have given a tenth that we actually start making an offering to the Lord. Richard Wurmbrand tithed his food in prison every 10th week.

Malachi 3:10 says,

"Bring the whole tithe into the storehouse."

The storehouse is the local church. It is a good thing to give individual gifts to individual organisations but that often impoverishes the local church. The church cannot release adequate giving to worthy causes and it cannot release ministries into the Lord's service.

Those who tithe are expressing their faith in God in the most practical way possible. They are saying "I believe that the 90% which I have left after tithing has God's blessing on it. With God's blessing the 90% can purchase more than the 100% would, without his blessing." It takes faith to believe that. When our lack of faith controls our stewardship, we limit God's ability to bless us.

3. The principle of self-control.

You need to be disciplined in your spending. This means that we should only spend what God has made us accountable for. Avoid "impulse" buying. It is said that men are given to "impulse" buying on the larger items, e.g. cars, computers etc. Women, on the other hand, impulsively buy the smaller things like clothes, make-up etc. In order to avoid overspending and impulse buying, you need to draw up a budget so that you ensure your income is greater than your expenditure.

The amount you earn is not important here; it's the discipline of staying with the limits of your income. Professionals who earn more than £100,000 a year sometimes have to ask for help because they have overspent. Make sure you account for everything in your budget – one off yearly payments, clothing emergencies, doctor's prescriptions, tithes, offerings etc. Build in a projected figure for all this and make sure your total remains within your income for the year. If it doesn't, go back and work on the figures again and revise downwards the cost of that expensive holiday.

Be wise in the use of credit and credit cards. The Bible never says that all debt is a sin, but it warns against it because many people do not use credit wisely. The key here is to make sure the project is a worthy one (e.g. buying a home, setting up a business, sending a child to college etc).

Then, you need to make sure you can afford the repayments and that they fit within your budget. Remember that when you take out a mortgage on a first home, as well as the monthly repayments, you will have running costs, repairs, decoration costs, insurance, utility bills to take into consideration.

4. The Principle of Saving

Saving is not for the purpose of bailing you out on a "rainy day." Someone said, "Don't save for a rainy day because you will then certainly get one." You need to save for those elements of your budget that occur annually – putting aside a percentage each month to cover the payment when it is due. You need to save for future goals such as the education of your child, buying a new car etc.

This will reduce the need for borrowing at a future date and your money is working for you in the meantime by accumulating interest. Of course, you need to save towards your retirement. Get yourself a good financial advisor who will help you find the right pension plan for you. All this makes prudent financial sense.

Proverb 22:3 says,

"A prudent man sees danger and takes refuge, but the simple keep going and suffer for it."

DEBT

Follow the principles laid down in this part of the book and it will help you avoid falling into debt. What is debt and is all debt morally wrong? Being in debt means that you are in a situation where you cannot afford the minimum repayments on a loan.

The repayments would cause you undue hardship. This of course means that not all debt is morally wrong, only debt that causes you undue hardship in repaying. If you are in debt, here's what you can do:

1. Recognise who owns your finances and hand them over to Him. Repent of taking matters into your own hands. You need to be humble enough to recognise that it's not by accident that you have got yourself into debt.

2. Determine to repay what you owe.
   "The wicked borrows, and pays not again; but the righteous deals graciously, and gives." (Psalm 37:21).
   You must establish the repayment of the loan as your number one priority. Don't take that expensive holiday while you are in debt. Use the money to reduce the amount you owe.

3. If you can, seek a "consolidation" loan from a reputable lender. This will bring all your debts under one lender who will extend the length of the loan, reduce the monthly interest and therefore reduce the amount of your monthly repayments. Some of the money released should be set aside for God.

4. Give to God in proportion to your ability in order to begin to experience God's blessing on the rest of your finances. The poor and those in debt need to give because they need the blessing of God to break the curse of poverty.

AREAS OF GIVING
Ways in Which you can Support your Local Church.

Tithing: Tithing (10%) is a starting point in our giving to God. It is an expression that all you have belongs to God. Remember to give a percentage of any "windfalls" you receive or any returns you receive on investments. By tithing on these, you are acknowledging that God's hand was behind your blessing.

Offerings: Offerings are anything you give over and above the tithe.

First Fruits: Give to God the first of any increase you receive i.e. salary increases.
"Honour the Lord with your wealth, with the first fruits of all your crops" (Proverbs 3:9).

Missions: You can give to missionaries and mission projects at home and overseas.

Other: From time to time there may be specific projects you can support such as the building fund.

May the contents of this message inspire you to release more of your wealth into working for the Kingdom.

CHAPTER 14

———— ❧ ————

THE VALUE OF KNOWING THE WILL OF GOD

Paul wrote:

"Therefore, I urge you, brothers and sisters, in view of God's mercy, to offer your bodies as a living sacrifice, holy and pleasing to God—this is your true and proper worship. Do not conform to the pattern of this world, but be transformed by the renewing of your mind. Then you will be able to test and approve what God's will is—his good, pleasing and perfect will" Romans 12:1, 2.

The word *"Approve"* as used in this scripture is derived the Greek word, Dokimadzo. It means to consider, or embrace after a thorough inspection.

- It means to inspect by walking through a situation – critically analysing every aspect of it in order to pass a recommendation.
- It carried the same idea as viewing several properties before settling for the one that passes the test – in terms of everything that you would consider acceptable about that particular property.

- It means to accept something based on careful observation and or discernment.

However, the Bible says we cannot establish the will of God for our lives by following the pattern set by the world. A pattern is a template. This meaning that the world has its set ways of doing things – its own template. But we Christians ought to follow the pattern set by God.

We do this by following the word of God.

When I was a young Christian I saw some people, also Christian, trying the find the will of God by using the patterns set by the world – plain Madness! Some simply flipped the Bible open, picked out the first verse that caught their eye and said that's it! I have found the will of God for my Life!

Some simply put a bible under the pillow at night hoping that by some spiritual form of osmosis, a scripture will leap into their minds while they are sleeping. Some would say, "I will know if this or that is God's will for me if a red car passes in front of me three times today. How silly is that? God's will is inextricably linked to His Word. So here's what I think we ought to do as Christians, to ascertain the will of God regarding any situation in our lives.

1. Approach God's Word prayerfully

Spend time in God's word prayerfully and meditatively. Avoid quick fixes. Remember,

"Trust in the Lord with all your heart and lean not on your own understanding; in all your ways submit to him, and he will make your paths straight" Proverbs 3:5,6.

You will be surprised at just how much God has to say about your job, family, your marriage, your kids, career etc.

2. Seek Godly Counsel

Especially from mature Christians – especially those in

leadership positions in your local church. To the Israelites of antiquity God said,

"Have faith in the LORD your God and you will be upheld; have faith in his prophets and you will be successful" 2 Chronicles 20:20.

Solomon also says,

"The way of fools seems right to them, but the wise listen to advice" Proverbs 12:15.

3. Do not go Round Forcing Words of Confirmation out of People.

Some people will tell you the very thing you want to hear from them. An incident recorded in Jeremiah 28:1-4, 15, 17 comes to mind at this point:

In the fifth month of that same year, the fourth year, early in the reign of Zedekiah king of Judah, the prophet Hananiah son of Azzur, who was from Gibeon, said to me in the house of the Lord in the presence of the priests and all the people:2 "This is what the Lord Almighty, the God of Israel, says: 'I will break the yoke of the king of Babylon. 3 Within two years I will bring back to this place all the articles of the Lord's house that Nebuchadnezzar king of Babylon removed from here and took to Babylon. 4 I will also bring back to this place Jehoiachin son of Jehoiakim king of Judah and all the other exiles from Judah who went to Babylon,' declares the Lord, 'for I will break the yoke of the king of Babylon.'"

15 Then the prophet Jeremiah said to Hananiah the prophet, "Listen, Hananiah! The Lord has not sent you, yet you have persuaded this nation to trust in lies. 16 Therefore this is what the Lord says: 'I am about to remove you from the face of the earth. This very year you are going to die, because you have preached rebellion against the Lord. 17 In the seventh month of that same year, Hananiah the prophet died.

Do not, using your own strength, try to open doors whose

time or season has not yet come. Psalm 37: 5, 6 says:

Commit your way to the Lord; trust in him and he will do this: He will make your righteous reward shine like the dawn, your vindication like the noonday sun.

And in Philippians 4:6 Paul says,

"Do not be anxious about anything, but in every situation, by prayer and petition, with thanksgiving, present your requests to God."

4. Commit Yourself Totally to God

When you are waiting on God to reveal his will, it is important that you yield to Him completely. Some Christians quickly start 'binding' and 'loosing' before they have even ascertained what the will of God is in whatever situation they may be in. His ways are not our ways.

Remember, the incident recorded in Acts 16:6-10. The Holy Spirit stood in the way of Paul and his ministry companions on their way to Asia Minor:

The Bible says:

Paul and his companions travelled throughout the region of Phrygia and Galatia, having been kept by the Holy Spirit from preaching the word in the province of Asia. 7 When they came to the border of Mysia, they tried to enter Bithynia, but the Spirit of Jesus would not allow them to. 8 So they passed by Mysia and went down to Troas. 9 During the night Paul had a vision of a man of Macedonia standing and begging him, "Come over to Macedonia and help us." 10 After Paul had seen the vision, we got ready at once to leave for Macedonia, concluding that God had called us to preach the gospel to them.

I must confess, waiting on God can be a frustrating exercise yet still, God knows best!

Psalm 37: 4 says,

"Take delight in the Lord, and he will give you the desires of your

heart."

To *"delight"* means to be pliable or flexible – to allow God to bend you towards the inclinations of His heart – not yours. Remember, how deceiving our human hearts can be.

5. Avoid Reading Scriptures by Vote (selectively) – based on how you feel.

God may want to bring correction to some area of your life as he leads you into His will but you may be saying, "I don't like this scripture, it does not relate to my situation."

Respect the authority of Scripture.

2 Timothy 3:16, 17 says,

"All Scripture is God-breathed and is useful for teaching, rebuking, correcting and training in righteousness, so that the servant of God may be thoroughly equipped for every good work."

And, in Hebrews 12: 5-7, we are told:

And have you completely forgotten this word of encouragement that addresses you as a father addresses his son? It says, My son, do not make light of the Lord's discipline and do not lose heart when he rebukes you, because the Lord disciplines the one he loves, and he chastens everyone he accepts as his son. Endure hardship as discipline; God is treating you as his children. For what children are not disciplined by their father?

6. Don't Get in the Habit of Throwing Fleeces at God

Christians sometimes have the tendency to try and twist God's arm for answers. "God, if this is really you, let me know by making my friend Craig or Zoe call me this afternoon at 4pm. don't take such chances!

The Bible talks about inner witness; one of them is the peace of God that passes all understanding – shall guard our hearts – Philippians 4:7 – not calls from friends and things like that. True peace in any given situation, negative or otherwise, is found when we run to the throne, not the phone.

The Bible says,

"If our hearts do not condemn us we have confidence before God" – *1 John 3:21*

Also, John 16: 13-15 says this:

But when he, the Spirit of truth, comes, he will guide you into all the truth. He will not speak on his own; he will speak only what he hears, and he will tell you what is yet to come. He will glorify me because it is from me that he will receive what he will make known to you. All that belongs to the Father is mine. That is why I said the Spirit will receive from me what he will make known to you.

7. Do not Try to Broker Deals with God

God cannot be bribed. He knows you better than you know yourself. Some people think that if they make a promise to God such as, "if you get my son out of this or that mess, I will help the poor" that He will get very excited and say, "in that case then I will grant your request very quickly!" No chance!

We need to understand saints that God is merciful – oh God is so nice – God is love. We didn't have to do anything apart from putting our faith in His son – Jesus – for us to be saved. Why are we trying to gain his favour now by trying to broker deals with Him? Scripture promises:

"I will not violate my covenant or alter what my lips have uttered" *Psalm 89:34.*

"God is faithful, who has called you into fellowship with his Son, Jesus Christ our Lord" *1 Corinthians 1: 9.*

"The one who calls you is faithful, and he will do it" *1 Thessalonians 5: 24.*

8. Check that your heart is right with God

Bitterness and vindictiveness can cause someone to make wrong choices. The sin of bitterness the bible says – develops roots – like the roots of a tree. They can eat into the whole of one's being to the extent that the very structure of their life starts to fall apart. It spreads and poisons the whole person. So many people are in a holding pattern today because of bitterness and unforgivenes.

What's a holding pattern you ask?

The English Dictionary's definition of a holding pattern is:

- A usually circular pattern flown by aircraft awaiting clearance to land at an airport.
- A state of waiting or delay; a static situation:

Ephesians 4: 30-32 says,

And do not grieve the Holy Spirit of God, with whom you were sealed for the day of redemption. Get rid of all bitterness, rage and anger, brawling and slander, along with every form of malice. Be kind and compassionate to one another, forgiving each other, just as in Christ God forgave you.

Spiritual frustration and unfulfilled spiritual desire should always in us asking for clarity of direction from God. Thus the hunger for more of God's presence must grow more intense than the spiritual supply. This should be the desire of every church and every child of God today.

Remember, "What you respect, you will always attract" – Mike Murdock

SEE YOU AT THE TOP!

More Books by Abraham A. Great
Available on Amazon

365 Brilliant English Words That Influence People

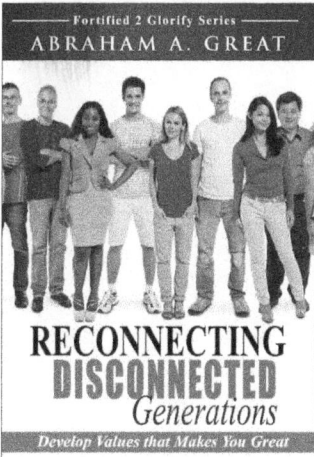

Reconnecting Disconnected Generations

www.ingramcontent.com/pod-product-compliance
Lightning Source LLC
Chambersburg PA
CBHW030418100426
42812CB00028B/3010/J